Keeping Students in Higher Education

Keeping Students in Higher Education

Successful

Practices &

Strategies for

RETENTION

DAVID MOXLEY, ANWAR NAJOR-DURACK
& CECILLE DUMBRIGUE

KOGAN
PAGE

First published in 2001

Kogan Page Limited
120 Pentonville Road
London
N1 9JN
UK

Stylus Publishing Inc.
22883 Quicksilver Drive
Sterling
VA 20166–2012
USA

British Library Cataloguing in Publication Data

A CIP record for this book is available from the British Library.

ISBN 0 7494 3088 5

Typeset by Jean Cussons Typesetting, Diss, Norfolk
Printed and bound in Great Britain by Biddles Ltd, Guildford and King's Lynn

Contents

PART IV   CONCLUSION

Dedication

With this dedication, we mourn the passing of our dear friend and colleague, Cecille Y Dumbrigue, whose struggle with breast cancer took her from us this year, well before her time, and well before her life mission was achieved. Many of the ideas and premises we offer in this book are of Cece's origination, knowledge garnered from decades of work with students of all backgrounds to facilitate their development and success.

Cece was an advocate of all students who sought higher education, which she viewed as one of the basic and most cherished opportunities a society could offer its people. Cecille frequently asserted that higher education should not be closed to those individuals who wanted to improve themselves and realize their potential as educated citizens, and who had something of value to give back to their communities.

For Cece, the purpose of higher education was to advance the common good and this meant that every successful student was yet another person who could undertake the arduous effort to improve the quality of life of her or his community. For Cece, higher education was a treasure, and she thought that no one could get enough of it. As a public educator, she facilitated the educational journeys of countless undergraduate and graduate students.

These basic beliefs most likely came from Cece's childhood experience with poverty and as a member of a minority group that often experienced discrimination. She overcame one barrier after another to complete her education and she never forgot these experiences and the people who helped her. She had a number of people who assisted her along the way, from primary school to graduate education, and she never forgot the legacy she vowed to uphold. She vowed to believe in others as her mentors believed in her and she perpetuated this legacy, one student at a time.

Cece constantly sought out students who were experiencing difficulties and she reached out to potential students to smooth their path to higher education.

Her ideas of student outreach, partnerships among community agencies and institutions of higher education, mentoring, student advocacy and student development can be found in this book. Her career and life were testimony to what we mean in this volume by proactive retention. She made a craft of student retention and persistence.

The book is filled with Cece's stories about students and about those retention and student support services in which she found delight and inspiration. She always told stories about her students and amplified their strengths and their ability to use ingenuity to overcome barriers to the completion of their education. The inclusion of many of Cece's stories of student success, fortitude and persistence ensures that the book has a deeply human face.

Cecille, we love and miss you. Thompson Home is not the place it once was when you roamed the halls. We miss how your spirit filled the School of Social Work in the early hours of the morning and throughout the day. To paraphrase Van Morrison's line in *Tupelo Honey*: 'You are an angel of the first-degree.'

David P Moxley and Anwar Najor-Durack
The Wayne State University School of Social Work at Thompson Home
Detroit, Michigan
20 May 2001

Introduction:
the practice of retention

A WELCOME TO OUR READERS

Welcome to our book, *Keeping Students in Higher Education: Successful practices and strategies for retention*. Its principal focus is the practice of retention, which means, in less technical language, keeping students in higher education. Readers of this book are likely to come from many different countries, backgrounds and perspectives, and to be very diverse in their perspectives on retention. Yet, all probably share something in common that brings them to this book: *a commitment to helping students to find their way to higher education, to helping them build the confidence and capacities to persevere toward their educational goals, and to helping them to be successful in their education, in their careers and ultimately in their lives.*

We assume that our readers come from many walks of life and from many backgrounds. Some may be teaching staff in community colleges, technical schools, research universities, traditional universities or 'new' universities. Some may be in undergraduate education or in post-graduate or professional education. Other readers may be specialized academic counsellors, staff members of community education courses and teachers working in adult education or continuing education courses. Others may be administrators responsible for student retention, while others may be departmental or course leaders who want to retain students and to maintain strong enrolments.

We also assume that there may be some readers who are not the traditional actors in retention but who nonetheless recognize the important roles they do play or want to play in keeping students in higher education. Included here may be those responsible for staff development or training, as well as members of community groups, members of the helping professions based in youth

1

development and social services agencies, members of the clergy and families of students. These individuals may find themselves increasingly involved in retention as practitioners who encourage students, mentor them and help them to troubleshoot and resolve personal, family or resource issues that can disrupt students' involvement and success in higher education. Keeping students in higher education is not limited and should not be limited to only specialized personnel based in post-secondary or higher education. Many people are relevant to retention. There is ample opportunity for strong partnerships among many different people, both within and outside higher education, who can make retention relevant and responsive to students to take them beyond the level of secondary school. Finally, it is also worth stressing that readers may be based in any country. Keeping students in higher education is an issue for all higher education systems, and while there may be specific local or national needs or priorities, policies or approaches, at its root the approach taken in this book is meant to be international.

THE PURPOSE OF THE BOOK

We do not want to offer a rigid framework for retention in higher education. We recognize that there is considerable variation in retention practices and strategies, and therefore we do not want to lock our readers into a framework that is too restrictive. Rather, we want to offer sensitive and responsive alternatives and perspectives. Retention is complex and we believe it is inappropriate to offer a simple, cookbook kind of approach to an area that is so rich. However, we feel a responsibility to capture the essence of retention in this volume. This is especially important since higher and post-secondary education is increasingly diverse. This diversity is expressed both in terms of the students and in terms of the sheer number and variety of educational courses, organizations and institutions around the world that now populate the post-secondary and higher education arena.

As practitioners of retention in higher education we feel a responsibility to chart out how educators, administrators, members of student development staffs, student leaders, community leaders and family members can help students to be successful academically, socially and personally in one of the greatest responsibilities of a person's life, that is, in defining a life and career direction through higher and post-secondary education, and moving into adulthood as a contributing citizen of a local community, a country and the world, and as a well-educated and well-prepared person.

We, ourselves, are diverse, and bring many different experiences to the project of retention in higher education. However, we share a core commitment to keeping students in higher education through means that respect the distinctiveness and full potential of each and every student. We look behind the statistics of retention to inquire into practices and strategies that any institution of higher or post-secondary education can use to assist its students to achieve success in their educational pursuits and in their educational and personal aspirations. So, let us introduce ourselves:

- *Anwar Najor-Durack* is of Chaldean heritage. She went to the United States with her family who emigrated from Iraq to find safety and opportunity. Anwar earned her first and post-graduate degrees in an urban research university where she now practises as an academic counsellor responsible for individualizing and customizing the retention efforts of a university department of social work. Anwar seeks to help her students to achieve success in post-graduate education and to assist them to be effective professionals. She keeps students in higher education by tailoring retention to the individual aims of each student.
- *Cecille Dumbrigue* was of Asian descent. Her family went to the United States to obtain economic opportunity and she was the first in her family to attend university, obtain a degree and then achieve a professional degree. She was head of marketing, admissions and advice of a university department of social work and she worked hard to make the department responsive to a diverse student population. Cecille said that making the department a learning community will enable all students to link their heritage to their educational aims. She believed that the essence of retention is to help students to discover what they want to achieve, and then to help them organize their situations so they can achieve their aims.
- *David Moxley* is of European ancestry. His parents' parents went to the United States to escape persecution. He was the first in his family to earn a PhD, something he was encouraged to do from a very early age. Indeed, his family was instrumental in fostering his own retention from the beginning of undergraduate education through to the completion of his post-graduate professional education. David recognizes how important it is for professors to take an interest in all students, to discover their career and personal aspirations, and to create learning opportunities that enable them to make progress towards their vision and dreams.

We, the authors, come from very different backgrounds. We point this out because each of us has a distinctive perspective on retention formed by our current educational roles, our educational experiences, and our family and ethnic experiences. All three of us come to higher education on different pathways. But, we agree on one thing. Keeping students in higher education is one of the most important roles educators can take today. The partnership we have formed convinces us that retention really does take a melding of different talents, roles and resources to help all students to be successful according to their own definitions of success.

Our own retention practice reminds us repeatedly that there are no 'quick fixes' to the achievement of retention. Institutions of post-secondary and higher education can formulate plans, launch new innovations or screen students more carefully in order to select the ones that can 'make it', but our experience has been a harsh mentor in these affairs. When we place the plan before the individual student, we have found that our effectiveness in keeping students in higher education only wanes.

Thus, in all chapters, we offer vignettes about individual students who seek success in higher education at the same time as they face challenging personal and educational issues. These vignettes remind us of the importance of the 'lived experience' among students, and the individual, group and community factors that can become so influential in making retention a positive outcome in post-secondary and higher education.

The plans and innovations are important tools. But they cannot replace a commitment to helping all students who come to post-secondary or higher education to sort out what they want for themselves. And, these plans cannot overlook the need to help all students to identify their own sense of vision and aspirations, and to address the personal, academic and resource issues that can become serious threats to continued persistence in education if left unaddressed and unresolved. In other words, the individual student is the unit of analysis of any successful retention effort. This book aims to offer readers ideas, tools and approaches that are relevant to helping one student at a time but that can also be combined and organized into a larger-scale plan.

Retaining the student: five vignettes

Retention must speak to each student, and involve the student directly in the process and outcome of retention. Students increasingly come to higher and post-secondary education from diverse backgrounds, and the challenge to us, as educators and as concerned professionals and community members, is to ensure that education and retention are responsive to this diversity. We offer five very short examples of this diversity from our own university experience to underscore how different student situations can influence the substance and aims of retention:

- John comes from a middle-class family and community. The majority of his school peers go on to enrol on full-time courses at colleges or universities. Many then go on to post-graduate or professional study after graduation. Despite John's strong secondary record, he comes to university with no clear sense of his academic aims. By the middle of his first year, he is in crisis. His parents are very disturbed by his poor academic performance and lack of what they call 'commitment'. John is despondent about his future. He wants help but doesn't know how to ask for it. And, no one reaches out to help him to make the critical decisions that are so important to his immediate situation and to his future.
- Sally has dreamt of higher education since her teens, but resigned

herself to not attending. She always thought that she was too poor and too ill prepared to get into college or university and to be successful in her educational choice. Next year, at the age of 51, Sally will graduate with a Master's degree in education. Her under-graduate work was tough but she completed it at the age of 49, and her post-graduate education was challenging. According to Sally, her tutor and faculty mentor made all the difference in the world. 'She hung in there with me, and did not give up. She always offered me solutions.'

- Hodja came to university as the first in her family to go on to higher education. She has strong and focused aspirations. Her aim is to become a dentist but she knows that she will have to balance study with full-time employment. Fortunately, her college has a deep commitment to co-operative education. Hodja can balance classroom work with co-operative work experiences.
- Mirna's family situation prevents her from enrolling full time as a student. At the age of 17, she is looking at about a six-year commit-ment to achieving a first degree. Mirna's strategy is to enrol in community college for three years and then transfer these credits to a university. She does not have much money and she needs to make sure that each credit transfers and counts towards her dream of a degree. But, the university to which she plans to go does not give her a clear sense of what can or cannot transfer.
- Lloyd comes to the university as a bright and energetic student, but his tutors soon discover that he does not write well. He gets criticized repeatedly for his weak writing ability, and he fails several courses because he cannot find an alternative way to demonstrate what he is learning. Lloyd withdraws from university feeling defeated. He says that he is not 'cut out' for higher education.

These five vignettes underscore the importance of each student situation, and how a retention effort must respond to each situation. The situations illustrate that retention is not only a matter of addressing the core academic skills of students. It is much more than this, even though each student must achieve acad-emic requirements to persist and to graduate. A mentor of one of the authors once said that post-secondary and higher education is such a challenging period since it is the time that 'students must come to grips with who they are and where they are going'. There is a strong element of personal responsibility and readiness to retention that any effort to keep students in higher education must respect and factor into the process.

But, as several of the vignettes illustrate, each student can benefit from a support system that the institution of post-secondary or higher education makes available so he or she can navigate the challenges inherent in the situation. Linking personal responsibility and enlightenment to support is a powerful way of keeping students in higher education. Thus, when we speak about retention in this volume, we often refer to the 'situation of retention' and the issues, barriers and needs that practitioners must address in each student's life situation. Diversity of student situations requires individualization, and perhaps even customization.

The vignettes that we incorporate into each chapter derive from our own retention practice. We use these vignettes in order to offer a strong flavour of these student situations, and to illuminate how retention policies, plans of action and encounters with students can be responsive in a manner that helps all students to achieve an outcome that makes sense to them and for them.

SPECIFIC AIMS OF THE BOOK

Our purpose in preparing this book produces six specific aims that we seek to achieve. These are to:

1. outline a basic approach to keeping students in higher education that practitioners can use to create their own approach to retention in post-secondary and higher education;
2. develop the nuances of this framework by examining qualities of discrete aspects of retention;
3. ground readers' understanding of retention through the use of substantive vignettes that illuminate how to be responsive to different student situations and different educational contexts;
4. expand readers' understanding of specific aspects of the development of retention programmes;
5. expand readers' understanding of the process of working with individual students to keep them in higher education;
6. help readers to apply the book's content to the creation and/or advancement of their own institutional retention efforts.

ORGANIZATION OF THE BOOK

Adopting a student-centred approach, this book explores numerous aspects of retention. We move from 'macro' considerations to 'micro' ones. In the early parts of the book, we consider institutional aspects and capacities in the framing of a responsive retention effort. In the middle parts of the book, we examine considerations pertaining to retention programmes and their development. The book then arrives at working individually with all students to help each one make those decisions that are crucial to his or her success.

For us, ultimately, retention is the process of helping all students to find their own pathway within the institution of post-secondary or higher education, and to muster the resources they need to travel this pathway to an outcome that they value. We recognize that although there are common elements to all educational institutions, retention requires the 'teaching of the culture of the institution' because each institution is unique in its traditions, values and mission.

Our student-centred approach to retention recognizes the importance of linking the self-discovery and self-definition of each student to higher education. As the great psychoanalyst Victor Frankel asserts, people can master situations when they understand what they want to become. Retention, for us, is a very 'hope-fulfilling' process.

A student-centred approach also means that institutions may need to let go of students if students decide that post-secondary or higher education is not for them at this time in their lives. How students leave educational institutions may influence whether they return. Students' different conceptions of themselves offer different implications for their academic persistence and retention. A sound decision about leaving and formulating a plan to return can advance the maturity of students, and it can enable them to understand the experience of post-secondary or higher education not as a failure but as a positive personal event in their development.

A retention effort can also keep the door open, and prepare students for future re-entry into post-secondary or higher education. The diversity we present in this book also recognizes that there are now different times within the human lifespan appropriate to entry into education. The idea that one pursues post-secondary or higher education only immediately after secondary education is no longer valid. We take the idea of lifelong education, adult education and continuous knowledge development seriously as the emerging norm governing student participation in post-secondary or higher education.

SPECIFIC CONTENT

The book is organized into four major thematic sections that move from institutional and higher-level considerations of keeping students in higher education to course-based considerations and then to considerations that pertain to working with individual students. In Part I (The challenge of retention), we offer a framework of retention in Chapter 1 and in Chapter 2 we explain how this framework is applied as a psychosocial intervention.

Part II (The institutional framework of retention) examines the specific properties of the institutional retention mission and offers readers criteria useful to the development of their own sense of mission, or to the appraisal of their current missions. This content is incorporated into Chapter 3. The content of Chapter 4 broadens the mission of retention as well as the retention effort to include both the internal community of post-secondary and higher education, and the communities to which the institution relates. This chapter helps readers to appreciate the many assets that these communities can offer to the retention effort, and to keeping students in higher education. Chapter 5 focuses on the infrastructure of retention and how this infrastructure is relevant to the support of students. Chapter 6 further develops the idea of student support and development.

The five chapters of Part III (Five dimensions of retention programmes) use new and previous content to identify and develop the various dimensions practitioners need to consider in the creation of their own retention effort. We examine the key dimensions of scope, auspices, outreach, roles and helping processes, and illustrate how each one can contribute to an effective retention effort and/or programme.

The single chapter we include in Part IV (Conclusion) enables us to bring the previous content together into a substantive example of a retention programme based on the best practices we illuminate in the book. We use this chapter to integrate the content of the previous chapters, and to consider the major phases and related activities that programme developers and those responsible for programme administration must address.

Part I
The challenge of retention

Keeping students in higher education: a pathway for retention

MAIN POINTS OF THE CHAPTER

- Basing retention on an institutional–community–student partnership will facilitate keeping students in higher education.
- Post-secondary or higher education courses use this partnership to become proactive in the retention of students, which is preferred to a reactive approach.
- There is considerable variation in the needs of students and this requires all retention efforts to be personalized to their needs.
- Although a programmatic framework is essential to proactive retention, the essence of keeping students in post-secondary or higher education lies in offering all students a set of personal relationships on- and off-campus that helps them to address the issues they face. Leaving these issues unresolved can force students to discontinue their education.
- Meeting the needs of students and helping them to overcome the issues they face as students requires the creation of student support systems that integrate the resources students need to move on in their education successfully.
- The principal aim of proactive retention is to help each student to learn the role of the student and to master the expectations and requirements that compose this role through a support system that is relevant to their needs and that helps them to achieve their aspirations.
- The pathway of retention achieves the following objectives. It enables a course of higher education to perceive a need for keeping its students, establish the importance of retention, create partnerships to support the

> success of students, offer a diversity of programmes to support student persistence, develop all students so they can achieve their aspirations, and monitor and track the status of all students and respond to them based on their situation and needs.

On the face of it, keeping students in higher education is not so difficult. At least this is what some readers may argue. It requires an institution of post-secondary or higher education to be certain that its students can meet the academic challenges its courses pose. It requires students to be 'good' students, ones who prepare themselves to meet academic challenges and who possess the maturity to use their strengths and to address and/or rectify their needs or deficiencies. But readers will see in the forthcoming chapters that retention is not this straightforward. We certainly agree that ultimately retention involves academic outcomes and the need for students to achieve these outcomes.

We underscore throughout these chapters, however, that retention is a complex personal, social and academic enterprise. It requires an institutional–community–personal partnership. This partnership links students to proactive support systems that a school or college customizes to help students to find a direction, evaluate their situations and meet those factors that can potentially disrupt their academic careers or even push them out of higher education or post-secondary education completely. Retention should not be reactive, only coming into play when a student is falling short of expectations or demonstrating deficiencies in substantive academic areas.

Underpinning this institutional–community–personal partnership is a conceptual pathway many institutions of higher or post-secondary education and their practitioners of retention can find useful. As noted in the introduction, it is not the intention of this book to be excessively prescriptive. Yet, we want to communicate the principal components and elements of this pathway with the hope that readers will find it useful in their own practice, and in their own efforts to create an approach to retention characterized by its innovative use of institutional and community resources, responsiveness to students and effectiveness in keeping students in higher education.

This chapter has three aims. First, it presents a negative example of the failure to keep a student in higher education. This sketch is given to illustrate the fact that increasingly students come to higher or post-secondary education with many different needs, and variations in their levels and types of supports. And, as a result, these students can present broad variations in the situations they deal with. Such students whose situations go unnoticed, unappreciated or unaddressed will probably fail to persist and this failure will probably result in the departure of these students from higher education. Second is a positive example of successful retention, not only to underscore the complexity of keeping students in higher education, but more importantly to show the power of a proactive approach to retention that a sound institutional–community–student partnership can produce. Finally, from these extended illustrative examples comes a conceptual framework that illuminates the pathway underpinning retention.

While both of the following examples use a student with psychologically driven retention needs, other needs could easily be substituted, such as family-driven problems, illness or disability, financially driven problems or other more straightforward motivational problems.

A NEGATIVE ILLUSTRATIVE EXAMPLE

Charlie's background

Twenty years ago, Charlie met the profile of an exceptional student. His grades in secondary education showed that he would be a good candidate for admission to a good university. His parents were fully behind him, and their own educational background and their aspirations for Charlie were strong. Charlie's education, however, was postponed by some dramatic events.

Charlie was an introvert and somewhat of a recluse. He did not have many friends at school, and was somewhat preoccupied with what his parents considered to be philosophical questions about life. They dismissed the seriousness of these 'traits' and took pride in his academic accomplishments. Charlie enrolled in a university far from home. His academic performance in his first term was marginal and his social adjustment was problematic. In the second term, he experienced a full-blown psychotic episode resulting in his hospitalization. His parents were devastated. The psychiatrist recommended that he should drop out of university, and that he and his parents should lower their expectations for what he would be able to achieve in both the short and the long run. He was preoccupied and withdrawn, and his parents found his delusions frightening.

Charlie experienced an abrupt role change. He was quickly transformed from promising student to psychiatric patient. At the age of 18 he started a new career that included multiple hospitalizations, involvement in outpatient medical and social care, and numerous frustrating attempts to hold on to jobs, housing and friendships. By the age of 25, his family had drastically reduced their expectations of him, and his psychiatric treatment team considered him to have a serious psychiatric disability. They warned him to reduce and control his stress and they continued to indicate that higher education was too stressful and something that was unlikely to be in his future.

Charlie's plan for higher education

But this is not the negative part of the example. We now flash forward some 18 years from the onset of his illness. Charlie is now 36 years old. His psychiatric illness is stable. He has benefited greatly from an excellent psychiatric rehabilita-tion programme. This programme helped him to achieve some medical stability, and his symptoms are well under control. He has many more good days than bad ones, even though he experiences some serious setbacks. He is a member of a psychiatric rehabilitation centre that he finds to be very supportive and helpful in practical ways. He has met Cindy, a staff member, on several occasions to clarify his educational aspirations. He wants to return to college and become a student again, and finds Cindy very positive and supportive. She notes that Charlie feels strongly about this and that he certainly has the assets and supports to begin to move ahead with his aspiration. Charlie and Cindy form a plan, and over a period of a year Charlie explores educational options available to him, and decides that the local college, Wilson Technological (a pseudonym), is the place for him to start.

Charlie enters college

But the college is not prepared for Charlie, and this is the negative part of the illustrative example. Charlie is a unique person, with unique experiences. But he is also a member of a group of people who need attention and consideration because of their backgrounds. They represent a pool of potential students who require a responsive set of supports from the college. Wilson Technological, however, does not recognize the need to accommodate its courses of study to the needs of a person with Charlie's background. The college does not perceive a need for a proactive approach to retention for this group of students and does not even identify the group as a legitimate one. The retention policy of the college is quite narrow, and it takes a traditional approach to retention. It is concerned with helping students with academic weaknesses to rectify these and to address substantive deficits in students' academic records. Retention for Wilson Technological amounts to academic preparation and academic follow-through.

Charlie is anxious about his enrolment. He is not really certain about his acad-emic direction, and his long psychiatric illness has battered his self-confidence. He knows that he has some 'odd mannerisms' and that he has difficulty asserting himself. He also knows that he is very vulnerable to stress and that academic expectations and requirements could potentially create some setbacks in his health. Once his tutor and other staff members know this background, Charlie is sure that he will be seen as an unsuitable student. He gets some encouragement from the staff members at the psychiatric rehabilitation centre but they also tell him he must accept that this is how higher education operates.

Charlie's personal tutor is not very positive about his future as a student, thereby confirming Charlie's fears. The tutor notes that Charlie's psychiatric background is a liability and that 'he needs to act correctly in order to make it as a student'. This is before the tutor shows any interest in Charlie's reasons for enrolling at the college or in his educational aspirations. The message from the tutor is consistent with the message the staff members at the psychiatric rehabilitation centre offer: 'You need to accommodate to the institution; it is not the other way around.'

Charlie is on his own

The tutor does not inquire into Charlie's assets, which are many: 1) his obvious motivation; 2) his desire for education; 3) his readiness as a student; 4) his bright intellectual functioning; 5) the self-management of his health; 6) the stability of his housing situation; and 7) the strong support he has from his rehabilitation team. The tutor does not think about how to use and complement these assets through the formation of an on-campus individual support system. The tutor refers Charlie to the college's office of disability services, but when Charlie goes to this office to inquire into the resources it offers, he is told that the students it serves have physical or learning disabilities. The counsellor at the office discourages Charlie's involvement and expectations for support, advising that they do not usually work with people with psychiatric problems.

Charlie's tutor enrols him in the basic educational curriculum in preparation for eventual transfer to a local university. He leaves it up to Charlie to do everything else since he does not want to treat him any differently from any other student. Charlie is petrified. Somehow he muddles through registration and basic student orientation. He arrives for the first day of class frightened, stressed out and depleted. At the meeting of his first class, Charlie asks a great many questions and behaves in what the teacher describes as an 'inappropriate manner'. The teacher is upset and openly confronts Charlie in class. Charlie leaves class and returns home. He isolates himself, fails to attend any of his classes and cuts off contact with the psychiatric rehabilitation centre. He does not drop his classes, and does not receive a refund. At the end of the term, he receives an academic report with three failing grades. He believes that he can't make it in higher education.

Some readers may say that this is an unusual situation. However, it occurs often in higher and post-secondary education. One view is that people with these kinds of backgrounds are not suited to the stress, ambiguity and self-direction higher education creates. Some readers may assert that Charlie is not ready for higher education. Others may assert that he will never be ready, and that higher education is not for everyone. Our view is that Charlie is a fine candidate and he is ready to become a student. However, is Wilson Technological ready to support him? Is the institution ready to help him master the role of student successfully?

A POSITIVE ILLUSTRATIVE EXAMPLE

Reframing the situation

We can reframe this situation, and illustrate a positive or proactive example here. The logic of retention calls for an institutional–community–student partnership and it is this kind of collaboration that can serve Charlie quite well. The responsibilities for persistence on Charlie's part cannot be dismissed. His mastery of the student role is vital to his educational success. And we must bring into the equation the psychiatric rehabilitation centre whose staff see Charlie's involvement in higher education as an important personal aspiration on his part. But we cannot and should not dismiss the role of Wilson Technological. The orientation of its policies, courses and staff to address Charlie's situation is critical to his success and to the success of students or potential students who find themselves in similar situations. How can Charlie be retained? How can Wilson Technological support his persistence?

Collaborative partnership to support Charlie's persistence and retention

Let's start with Charlie's interaction with the staff of the psychiatric rehabilitation centre. He comes to the tentative decision on his own that he wants to return to higher education. He takes the risk to reveal this to Cindy, the staff member at the centre. She reviews the assets and strengths Charlie has in place to support this decision and the two of them, in collaboration, reflect on Charlie's motivation, aspirations and specific aims. They note the progress he has made in his rehabilitation, and the stability he has achieved in his health and medical position. He is also pleased with his current housing situation. He recently experienced a setback in his functioning, but he and his treatment team quickly addressed the setback and he got back on track. One outcome of this setback is that Charlie learnt about several stressors he needs to reduce and control in order to continue to lead a lifestyle he finds satisfying. He learns that these stressors must be managed so he can become a successful student.

Charlie and Cindy agree to meet four times to explore his interest in higher education. At the third meeting, Cindy spends time orienting Charlie to the educational options he has available to him. She notes that the psychiatric rehabilitation centre and Wilson Technological have a collaborative relationship to help students with backgrounds similar to Charlie's to 'be successful in higher or post-secondary education and training of their own choosing, and to help them to master the role of student successfully'. Cindy suggests that they meet a tutor at Wilson Technological so that Charlie can hear directly what the college can offer him and how they support his choice.

Cindy has a great deal of confidence in Wilson Technological. The chief academic officer of the college commissioned a task force of college and community representatives to offer input on the retention mission of the college, and to identify groups of potential students whose retention needs demanded new competencies on the part of the college. Representatives from the psychiatric rehabilitation centre participated in this needs assessment, planning and mission-writing project. The participation resulted in the identification of people with psychiatric disabilities in the mission statement, and in a mutual collaborative technical assistance project between the college and the centre, supported by a government grant. This project resulted in an enhancement of the ability of the college to interact in an effective and supportive manner with potential and enrolled students with mental health backgrounds. Cindy knows that the tutor they are to meet has a strong commitment to helping students with mental health needs to be successful as students.

Charlie develops his readiness for higher education

Charlie is very anxious about the arranged meeting. He misses the appointment, and Cindy contacts him by telephone to discuss the situation. She reassures him that this is merely an exploratory meeting for him to get to know the tutor and something about the college. They reschedule for the next day. The relaxed demeanour of the tutor impresses Charlie, who gives every reason why he is not a good candidate. These do not reduce the tutor's confidence in the aspiring student. The tutor's gentle tone and warmth help Charlie to understand the challenges he will need to meet in order to achieve his aspiration of becoming a student in the college. The tutor invites Charlie to lunch so that he can meet another student and a staff member who have similar backgrounds to his own. At lunch he is quite withdrawn. However, he agrees to shadow the student for the day. He calls Cindy the next day and says he wants to become a student.

The college organizes special orientations for students with different concerns, needs and situations, for example female students and students with family responsibilities. Charlie attends the orientation for students who have been out of education for some time. The orientation gives him basic information about the support systems the college offers and how to take advantage of different courses. A representative from the office of disability services offers him an alternative. He can participate in an extended orientation lasting one full term that will help him to achieve four objectives:

1. Gain an understanding of student role expectations and receive ongoing support through a student-led educational support group.
2. Make the transition into the role of student through involvement in a seminar on how college works, study skills, student–staff relations and career development.
3. Meet and socialize with other students of similar backgrounds.
4. Obtain detailed information about the resources of the college, and complete the steps the college requires of prospective students, covering financial issues and an assessment of academic assets.

Cindy also suggests that Charlie visit the weekly student dinner the psychiatric rehabilitation centre offers members who are returning or who want to return to education. The dinner offers participants an opportunity to discuss and address issues they face in mastering the role of student. It is co-led by a staff member of the centre, a student member of the centre and a staff member of a local college.

Charlie elects to enrol in the extended student orientation. He is impressed with the personal control he has over his educational experience in that he can dictate how quickly he wants to go through the process and what he wants to address. His tutor understands Charlie's situation and background and, more importantly, understands what Charlie wants to achieve. The tutor is flexible and willing to help Charlie with almost anything he brings to him. Charlie has a support system both on- and off-campus that is there to help him identify and troubleshoot the issues he faces.

Charlie receives support for academic performance

Completing the extended orientation prompts some anxiety in Charlie. He wants to move on and enrol formally but he is uncertain whether he can do this. His college tutor does not hear from him and contacts him at home. The tutor suggests to Charlie that he ease into coursework by trying two courses this term, and Charlie decides to take a demanding course and an easier one. By the second week of the new term, he is not doing well. He does not act appropriately in class and his behaviour prompts a member of staff to ask him for a meeting. The member of staff has taken part in the college training programme on retention and views his step as a proactive one. Charlie's tutor and Cindy are also present at the meeting. The three of them are able to help Charlie reduce his anxiety, and they all contribute to a plan that will help him to learn the role of student. During the course of the term, Charlie needs several of these meetings, and the member of staff and tutor treat them as a normal part of becoming a student at the college. Charlie chooses to continue with his on-campus support group and to attend the student dinners at the centre once a month.

From time to time, he has some setbacks. Once he misses an entire term. Another time he misses three weeks of a term. The scope of the college's retention programme is broad enough to help him navigate all of these academic, personal and career challenges. Indeed, as he progresses in his course, he takes advantage of a number of informal career development offerings. His ongoing relationships with his tutor and with Cindy help him to explore opportunities in the life sciences, engineering and human services. He is beginning to consider a career in information technology.

Charlie's subjective sense of retention is very positive

Charlie finds the experience 'friendly and supportive'. He believes the members of his on-campus and off-campus support systems want him to be successful. The tutor, members of his peer support network, staff of the psychiatric rehabilitation centre and several members of staff at the college actively facilitate his involvement in a very informal manner. Charlie feels that he receives advocacy, mentoring, counselling and, when he needs it, crisis intervention. After three terms of part-time status, Charlie moves to full-time.

Features of an effective retention programme

Charlie's experience is indicative of an effective retention effort. There is an institutional and programmatic structure in place, but Charlie does not feel that he is treated in an impersonal manner. He experiences retention as if the institution set out to customize the approach specifically for him. In addition, he does not feel singled out in a negative sense. He senses that he is part of an institutional commitment to retention, and that he is a member of a group whose retention issues the college thoughtfully identifies and responds to in a sensitive and respectful manner. For Charlie, the pieces of the retention effort fit together, and he can, in turn, compose the retention effort that makes the most sense for him.

This extended example illustrates what we mean by an institutional–community–student partnership. However, the partnership does not hold promise for retention if there is any failure to personalize a student's situation. One of our principal hypotheses is that personalization works to strengthen and improve retention. Thus, even though Wilson Technological possesses an explicit programmatic approach to retention, what makes this programme work for Charlie is its personalized character. Witness how many times key relationships present themselves as assets in his educational situation. Cindy, the tutor, other students and members of college staff combine in ways that we cannot make all that explicit. Perhaps we must conclude that personal relationships make a retention programme effective. The countenance of retention is expressed through the people who make it happen on behalf of each and every student. In this manner, within the second example, Charlie's experience is not unusual. He finds that the institution's retention programme makes higher education work for him.

THE PATHWAY TO RETENTION: A CONCEPTUAL FRAMEWORK

All of the ingredients for a successful retention programme are found in this second, positive exemplar documenting Charlie's experience in college. Figure 1.1 offers a pictorial representation of these ingredients. It illustrates the substantive objectives of a retention programme, the outcomes a retention programme seeks and the critical elements that make the retention programme operate.

We must underscore that this figure only represents how the institution of post-secondary or higher education organizes retention. It does not represent how the student experiences retention, or how the retention effort is organized for a specific student. The following sections outline each part of the framework that the exemplar of Charlie's situation reflects:

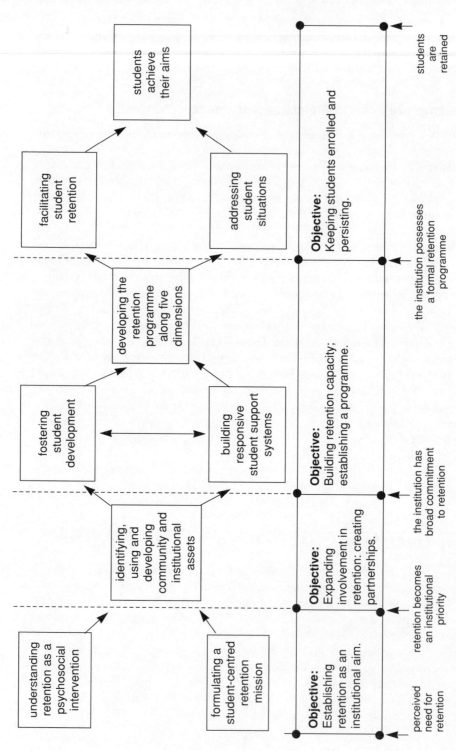

Figure 1.1 *Pathway to retention*

Objective 1: The institution of higher or post-secondary education perceives a need for retention

The negative exemplar clearly shows that Wilson Technological does not possess a strong sense of the need for a retention effort of broad scope. It does not fully understand Charlie's situation and needs and, as a result, fails to organize a pervasive, integrated and comprehensive approach to the group of students Charlie represents. The second or positive exemplar illustrates how an institution perceives this need. It reaches out to the internal and external communities to identify those groups that require attention through the process of retention. A retention needs assessment was important to setting the stage for Wilson Technological to work successfully with Charlie.

The needs assessment can help an institution of higher or post-secondary education to identify those groups that require outreach, support and attention in the process of persistence and retention. The outcome of this objective is that the institution possesses a clearer sense of who needs or requires retention, and offers the institution an understanding of the student situations that must be the focus of the retention programme.

Objective 2: The institution of higher or post-secondary education establishes retention as an institutional aim

The outcome of this objective is that retention becomes an institutional priority, and the importance the institution attaches to this priority expresses itself in a retention mission. We see the role of the retention mission inherent in the second exemplar of Charlie's situation. Charlie is not alone and isolated in his quest for educational success. Many different representatives of Wilson Technological are willing and able to reach out to him and support him in both formal and informal ways. The tutor, staff, students and community representatives all stand ready to work with him, and they are prepared to help him triumph over barriers that could otherwise defeat him. It appears from this exemplar that Wilson Technological treats retention as a priority, formulates a strong retention mission and understands that this mission must encompass a broad formal and informal approach to retention that involves the student, institutional representatives and community members. The retention mission of Wilson Technological appears to be student-centred and to require the college to personalize retention for each student.

The mission as acted upon by Charlie's tutor, teachers and peers recognizes the importance of his aspirations and goals as a student, and his need to master the role of student in a way that enables him to overcome the barriers his situation presents. In this manner, the mission suggests to the members of the Wilson Technological community that retention is a psychosocial intervention (see Chapter 2), that is, retention requires the bringing together of a student's aspirations and personal assets with a strategic approach to the reduction of the barriers the student experiences on- and off-campus and the use of supports that enable the student to master the role of student.

Objective 3: The institution expands involvement in retention and creates partnerships that support and contribute to the success of students

The negative exemplar we offer in this chapter reveals how disconnected the students' community supports can be from their institutional supports. Cindy encourages Charlie to try the role of student while the tutor at Wilson Technological seems to discourage him. The synergy of bringing these supports together for Charlie can be seen in the positive exemplar. Framed by a strong and positive retention mission, an institution of higher or post-secondary education can build on the involvement of community resources in the retention needs assessment by forming collaborative agreements between the educational institution and community groups or institutions. Each has something distinctive to contribute to retention as we see when Cindy becomes involved in helping Charlie to master the role of student.

Such collaboration broadens the priority the institution of higher or post-secondary education assigns to retention to encompass more of the community, more groups and individuals, and hopefully more resources to invest in keeping students in higher education. In Chapter 4, we illustrate how community partnerships and relationships can become part of the retention effort of the educational institution.

Objective 4: The institution builds a retention capacity and establishes a formal programme for keeping students in higher education

We witness in Charlie's situation how important his development as a student is to his mastery of the student role. He is quite anxious about this transition in his life and his psychological state can undermine his performance as a student. Fortunately, Cindy, the tutor and some of the college staff understand his situation and the many needs he experiences in order to make his transition to full-time student a successful and positive one. Institutional and community representatives have a lot to offer him so that he can be successful as a student.

There is a process the institution offers Charlie to induct him into the role of student. The extended, one-term orientation offers him an opportunity to ease into the role of student and 'learn the ropes' about how college works. The regular student dinner held by the psychiatric rehabilitation centre helps Charlie to learn informally about the student role through an active exchange with his peers who find themselves in similar situations. And there is a personal process that he can make use of through his tutor. The tutor encourages his development as a student by helping him to:

- explore academic opportunities;
- make decisions about what and how many courses he will take;
- create a plan guiding his subsequent academic work;
- identify and resolve barriers that can disrupt his work as a student;
- achieve outcomes that support his current and subsequent success.

Charlie exercises a great deal of control over this student development work. He sets the pace at which he will work and he modifies his workload and requirements to fit the realities of his personal situation and health. Although an institution of higher or post-secondary education stipulates requirements, increasingly students want, seek and perhaps even need flexibility, as Charlie so graphically illustrates for us. The personal process of student development, which, as we outline in Chapter 6, is often emotional and maturational, fits well with the formal courses the institution offers to strengthen study skills, literacy, numeracy and basic educational competencies of students. It is these formal courses that help students address their learning needs and eliminate or reduce those academic barriers that can threaten educational success. In Charlie's situation, he is able to link his personal development through supportive relationships with his academic development through an intensive term of academic orientation and preparation that offers him a solid retention opportunity as he progresses into the formal curriculum of the technological school.

The five dimensions of a retention programme

Wilson Technological has put in place all five major dimensions of a formal retention programme. The scope of the programme (Dimension 1) is broad enough to address both personal and institutional needs. The college's retention programme enables Charlie to address his own situation and his academic needs through an integrated approach to personal and institutional support. The programme has the capacity to integrate college and community resources, but its leadership is based in the institution of higher learning in the role of the tutor. Thus, there is a clear support structure for retention leadership and responsibilities (Dimension 2). However, the college does not isolate the programme in one area of the institution, but seeks to diffuse retention activities broadly through outreach, awareness building, information campaigns and educational development of staff (Dimension 3).

The individuals who provide retention support and services can engage in various types of retention roles to meet the individual needs of students. Thus, students can obtain advocacy, mentoring, counselling, crisis intervention or resource development from various people, as Charlie's situation illustrates in the second exemplar (Dimension 4). These helping roles can be brought together into one principal person or they can be shared among team members. Charlie had several people working with him so one person did not have to respond to all the situations he needed to address. While a college staff member or tutor could mentor him, Cindy was available to offer crisis intervention or counselling. A good retention effort, as the second exemplar illustrates, makes these roles available and accessible to students in a manner that does not require considerable effort or energy. The programme should operate in a smooth manner.

Although students may perceive and experience the retention programme as informal, it has enough formal structure and process to make it accountable and effective. Key processes of retention are put in place and implemented to offer students substantive supports and services. The key processes of retention (Dimension 5) include:

- initial contact and assessment, and the formulation of an outcome-based retention plan;
- an individualized support system;
- ways to troubleshoot the issues students face and must resolve;
- ways to put closure on retention and help students to link to the next steps in their education or career.

Processes should help students to contemplate the appropriateness of higher education for them and help them to get ready for the transition into the role of active student. Processes were in place to help Charlie to create an individualized support system that in his case was a team of individuals from college and community. When he had setbacks in his health, he was able to get back on track because there were people available to him to troubleshoot and resolve these issues. It is important to note that these individuals were committed to his success, and they did not frame any one issue as disqualifying Charlie from involvement in higher education. They framed any issue as something that they all needed to resolve so that Charlie could get on with his educational career. This is an essential quality of proactive support systems in retention.

Charlie's next step is to obtain the assistance of his college support system to plan the transition to his next educational experience, which will be to complete a degree. Part of the linkage and transition work of his team will be to help him form key relationships with individuals who can foster his persistence and retention at his next institution of higher education.

Objective 5: The institution keeps students enrolled and persisting towards the fulfilment of their educational aspirations and aims

What should be obvious in the framework we offer in Figure 1.1 is that retention does not have a narrow focus or address only academic preparation and the achievement of academic outcomes. Retention is a product of a number of different areas of a student's life, and the educational institution must be prepared to foster and/or facilitate development in these key areas. The partnership between Wilson Technological and Charlie started with the facilitation of readiness. The long period of time Charlie had been away from formal education, coupled with the issues his personal health situation created, meant that a good retention programme needed to help him to ease back into the student role. Without attending to his readiness and handling this as part of the retention process, he may never have engaged in or subsequently mastered the student role. The readiness process also illuminated his needs for academic development and personal development. He needed to gain an understanding of his approach to learning, his understanding of his health concerns and needs, and the supports available to him in and outside college that could help him to resolve the issues he faced in his course of study.

This personal development work ran parallel to his academic development work. For example, Charlie took advantage of the assessment process for identifying his academic strengths and needs, and this resulted in a programme of academic development that was tailored to his background, learning assets and substantive needs.

As Charlie became increasingly involved in his academic work, he started asking fundamental questions about why he should persist. He wanted to know what education would mean to him, what he could do with it and what he wanted to do with it. Answers to these questions were available through his retention programme. He explored professional and career options, and was able to identify a professional or career direction by the latter part of his time at Wilson Technological. He found helpful the part-time work opportunities, job shadowing experiences and career workshops held at the college and the psychiatric rehabilitation centre. These activities helped him to clarify his career interests and preferences, and enabled him to link his academic work to the professional direction he sought through his education. He gained a vision of what he wanted to become, and this helped give further meaning to his current and subsequent involvement in higher education.

Importance of a personalized approach

Thus the facilitation of retention incorporates readiness, academic development, personal development, and professional and career development. However, it is likely that such facilitation will not be undertaken independently of actual student situations. Each student brings to higher education a background formed from the influence of personal and family experiences, and economic, cultural and social forces. Charlie has a set of experiences and a situation that the educational institution must consider if it is to retain him as a student.

There are certainly many other situations, like those of women who come back to campus after long periods of absence or students with young children. Other situations again involve students who have experienced discrimination or economic and social disadvantage, or students who drop in and out of higher education in order to address or fulfil other needs or preferences, particularly economic ones. While we only address a limited number of these situations in subsequent chapters, sensitivity to the variety of situations and addressing them within the context of a retention programme through different strategies of facilitation will give a rich, differential character to an institution's retention approach. As Figure 1.1 indicates, students will probably achieve their educational aims if the programme addresses the substantive issues these situations create. The second exemplar we offer in this chapter shows how students can be successful if the educational institution is prepared to address the issues the student's situation creates through a personalized, differential and comprehensive approach to retention.

CONCLUSION AND GUIDELINES

The two illustrative examples we include in this chapter cannot be generalized to all retention situations. However, the principles, practices and strategies that the examples reflect certainly are applicable to many different educational contexts and situations requiring a sensitive approach to retention. Note how often the idea of support emerges within the illustrative examples. Indeed, we assert that keeping students in higher education involves a range of supportive practices and strategies that an educational institution applies to a number of different student situations. *By support we mean the matching of resources to the needs of students so that they can master the role of student and perform in a manner that brings them academic success as they and/or the educational institution define it.* The box below summarizes five forms of supportive retention practices. It is useful for us to identify these since they can underpin or contribute to a number of different programmatic approaches to retention.

FIVE FORMS OF SUPPORTIVE RETENTION PRACTICES

Emotional support and sustenance

- The programme recognizes that entry and involvement in higher education can cause considerable anxiety.
- The programme anticipates the stress students can experience and seeks to reduce this stress.
- Staff offer sympathetic understanding to students regarding the challenges they face and the stress these challenges can cause.
- The programme establishes a warm and supportive atmosphere that welcomes the involvement of students who may be experiencing retention challenges.

Informational support

- The programme assumes that many students may not understand the role requirement that higher education demands of them.
- Students get the information they need to fulfil their needs on campus.
- Students get access to other students who have been successful and who can give them informal information about how to make it in higher education.

Instrumental support

- Students can get practical assistance to resolve the educational challenges and issues they face.
- Students can get help with the problems or concerns they face in their daily lives such as in the areas of financial resources, housing, health and mental health care, and transportation.
- The programme offers students practical technical assistance and advocacy to persist in their education.

Material support

- Tangible financial assistance to support participation in higher education.
- Financial resources to support housing.
- Flexible loan arrangements.
- Retention loans and emergency assistance loans.

Identity support

- The programme recognizes the importance of helping students to strengthen their identities and to link persistence in higher education to support from staff and other students who share similar needs.
- Provision of self-help opportunities.
- Mutual support groups and community-building activities.
- Valuing of diversity and cultural affiliation.
- Opportunities to express identity through social and cultural activities.

These supports 'wrap around' students to support their academic achievement and success. This process is described in the following sections, using the example of Charlie.

Emotional support and sustenance

The people working with Charlie express positive emotional regard towards him. They are not judgemental about his background, and they accept and affirm his current aspirations as someone who is making important personal choices. The emotional support Charlie receives helps to strengthen his relationships with the people who can help him to achieve success as a student. And these relationships help him to reduce the anxiety and fear that could disrupt his involvement and performance in higher education.

Informational support

Charlie gets information about higher education at a rate and in a manner that he can process and use. What is notable about this information is that it comes both informally and from several sources. The psychiatric rehabilitation centre offers information about how to get involved in higher education, while the tutor at Wilson Technological gives him basic information about academic expectations. Charlie continues to get information about 'how college really works' from other students with backgrounds similar to his own, the members of the student dinner group at the rehabilitation centre and the members of the peer support group at the college. The information comes to him in a manner that does not overwhelm him.

Instrumental support

Charlie also receives support that helps him to solve the problems he experiences along the way to becoming a student, and to solve those problems he experiences when he formally enrols and performs as a student. We need to appreciate that the members of Charlie's support team treat the problems he experiences as ones that any student can experience, thereby normalizing the issues, barriers and concerns he faces. Charlie begins to understand that mastering the role of student and performing in a successful manner will create a number of different issues or problems, and he has people to whom he can turn for pragmatic advice, direction and even technical assistance. His support circle is broad and rich enough not to limit but to expand the problem-solving assistance available to him. He considers his tutor to be flexible and available but involves him only in academic matters. Cindy comes into play in helping him to manage personal problems. He looks to the members of the student dinner group to help with his frustrations about college, and his peer support group at college help him to learn about tutors, financial aid and academic requirements.

Material support

As Charlie moves further into his educational role, problems or crises may emerge pertaining to his financial stability, housing, transportation and other basic resources. The growing popularity of higher education among the members of the psychiatric rehabilitation centre prompts administrators to develop substantive material supports to facilitate educational access and involvement. These material supports include assistance with tuition, a small loan scheme that helps members to purchase books and materials, and a housing support scheme that assists members to obtain housing if they experience disruption. This material support enables students to lower their anxiety and address disruptions that can destabilize their involvement in higher education.

In real life, institutions can offer these kinds of flexible and innovative resources that can help students to address life events and issues that can potentially disrupt their persistence and retention. Tangible resources like expedited financial aid, flexible loan arrangements, provision of childcare, employment and employment advice, transportation, and health and mental health care are some of the material supports that an educational institution can offer its students.

A dramatic example of material support of students is found at a small college in the United States. The school's mission is to ensure that promising low-income residents of Appalachia have access to higher education. The college offers all students on-campus work options to reduce or subsidize the costs of their education. The employment scheme encompasses the production, marketing and sales of regionally inspired arts and crafts, the operation of major school facilities and the operation of a hotel.

Identity support

Charlie identifies himself as an 'ex-patient' and as someone in 'recovery'. He is not alone in his effort to make sense of his background, and to use it as a way of giving meaning to his educational experience and the challenges he faces in mastering the student role. Increasingly, contemporary students learn about themselves through personal experiences, therapy that illuminates their qualities, and self-help experiences that give meaning to who they are and what they had to overcome to achieve success as people and students.

Identity may encompass illness, substance use, sexual orientation, ethnicity, poverty and other social issues or labels. Of course, these are not all comparable experiences or issues, and support for identity helps all students to make decisions about how they want to create or fashion their own support systems based on their qualities, experiences and situations. This kind of support typically incorporates self-help and/or mutual support. Students with common experiences or who face common issues may come together to nurture and sustain one another. Self-help and/or mutual support enables students to interpret their experiences in the institution and to become sensitive to how well they are regarded or disregarded. Self-help and mutual support may offer opportunities for academic development through courses like women's studies, ethnic studies, gay/lesbian studies and disability studies. And self-help and mutual support may foster social action in the institution that enables students to address inequities or discrimination. In our example, Charlie's peer support group offers opportunities for him to address issues he faces as someone in recovery. He has been able to join with his peers to educate staff and other students about the realities of mental health and the needs of students who come to college as ex-patients or as mental health consumers.

Ultimately, from our perspective, educational persistence and retention is all about support. We show in this chapter that the pathway to retention involves the organization of supports for students at several levels of the educational institution, and involves the articulation of need, purpose, mission, programme and service. But, as we assert in subsequent chapters, retention really does involve assisting one student at a time to obtain the supports he or she needs or wants to help in embracing and performing the role of student successfully and effectively.

2

A student-centred approach to retention

MAIN POINTS OF THE CHAPTER

- Post-secondary and higher education are changing dramatically. New types of post-secondary education are emerging to fulfil the economic, cultural, social and service needs of both emerging and developing societies. This changing character of post-secondary and higher education in turn fosters a wide spectrum of student roles at all levels including developmental education, technical education, pre-professional education, undergraduate education, and post-graduate and professional education.
- As student roles proliferate and change, patterns of persistence change. Students now have a diversity of options for completing their education as higher education restructures to meet new demographic, economic and technological realities. Changes are occurring to the delivery of post-secondary and higher education in response to student role change including the use of technology to repackage courses and requirements, modification of ways credits are earned and the manner in which students demonstrate their proficiencies.
- At the same time as student roles are changing, students face a multitude of social and personal issues that intrude into the educational setting and influence the persistence and retention of students.
- To promote retention and persistence of students, higher education must appreciate the diversity of educational opportunities available to students and how they want to take advantage of these opportunities, student demographics and backgrounds, how students undertake their educational careers, and how students learn and achieve educational outcomes.

- Given the extent of social and economic change, students may need to approach their education at several different levels. It is not unusual for students to seek education to fulfil immediate situational employment needs, to prepare for specific careers, to make career transitions and to engage in lifelong education.
- The nature of this diversity requires post-secondary and higher education to understand the educational aspirations, aims and resources their students or potential students possess and the realities they face. Understanding this diversity sets the stage for a student-centred response to retention and persistence.
- A student-centred approach means that the institution of post-secondary or higher education responds to the educational aims of all students by helping them to get the tools they need, fulfil their needs and resolve the issues they face so that they persist in their education and achieve an educational outcome they value.

To define retention solely as a narrow educational issue belies many ways of thinking about and looking at this challenge in higher education. Indeed, retention requires staff, students and administrators in higher education to appreciate its broad scope. For higher education, these are changing times, as societies redefine the nature and substance of post-secondary education and training. No longer can we think of higher education as beginning with the traditional three- or four-year curriculum that students start immediately following secondary education and complete in the allotted time.

New patterns of higher education are emerging within the context of developing countries, post-industrial societies and postmodern communities. The three- or four-year, 'all at once' educational career no longer characterizes the undergraduate student. And those students who pursue post-graduate and professional education no longer follow the stereotype. Students do not necessarily move on to professional and post-graduate education immediately following the completion of their undergraduate work. They may volunteer, work full time, engage in other developmental or career exploration activities, or raise families as they prepare – emotionally, intellectually, financially and socially – to continue their academic careers, if indeed they choose to do so at all.

Students also face a multitude of social issues, and serious challenges to participation in and subsequent completion of a post-secondary or higher education course of studies. Personal issues that relate to educational background, opportunities, family, health, financial stability and even safety can play into the retention equation. Also, the pace of social change can bring about role change in personal relationships and families with the consequence that participation in higher education itself may cause family strain and conflict as students change their values, attitudes and sense of the world. Of course, we must also incorporate here the rapid pace of societal change. Changes within principal social institutions, particularly the economy and the world of work, create retention challenges. More than ever before, students must balance work, income and education and, as a consequence, they may need to prolong their educational career so that they can afford to complete their studies or training. The challenge of retention is indeed complex.

RETENTION AND DIVERSITY

Post-secondary education is now as diverse as the students who seek it. Five aspects of the diversity of post-secondary education are of particular importance to appreciating the idea of retention. These are:

- the diversity of post-secondary and higher educational alternatives and opportunities;
- the diversity of student demographics;
- the diversity of students' educational careers;
- the diversity of student learning;
- the diverse role education serves in the modern lifespan.

Diversity of educational opportunities

There are now more and more forms of post-secondary education so that traditional undergraduate and post-graduate courses are no longer the norm or no longer the sole options available to students. Technical schools, specialized vocational training institutes, community colleges, four-year liberal arts schools, research universities, open and distance learning, flexible adult education and even modern apprenticeships reflect only some of the sheer diversity of what is now available to students. This diversity offers students a range of opportunities as they think about their educational development, their personal growth and development, their employability and their prospects for career preparation or change. These alternatives raise issues about what is right for particular students in terms of their educational backgrounds, their current maturity and their aspirations. They raise issues about what form of higher or post-secondary education is a good match for a student, and this is a factor in his or her choice of institution as well as specific course.

We cannot ignore the role of information and educational communications technology that is rapidly changing the face of higher education. Increasingly students have options involving how to consume or otherwise participate in education. They can affiliate with several different institutions simultaneously as technology reduces the significance and influence of physical distance. Internet courses, online learning, distance learning, videoconferencing, knowledge-based systems and GroupWare are some of the technological alternatives that help and will help to package courses in different ways, change teaching and learning dramatically, and offer new ways of interacting among students and teaching staff. Technology offers many exciting options that can even redefine what educational institutions mean by student, persistence and retention.

Implied here is that the educational and personal assets and strengths, personal and social needs, perspectives, values and self-conception of the student are critical ingredients to producing this good fit. The diversity of post-secondary and higher educational options suggests that students need insights into what they are choosing and why they are choosing a specific educational option. Retention as an idea, and as a process of helping students to persist in their education, is linked to the fundamental idea of match and goodness of fit.

Diversity of student demographics

Students are probably now more diverse as a population than ever before. The demographics of students and potential students are changing at this writing, and they have changed tremendously over the past two decades. Students bring into educational settings considerable diversity in terms of age, gender, class, sexual orientation, race, ethnicity, and learning orientations and styles. Language, customs, traditions and ultimately culture combine to produce classrooms in which students from very different and diverse backgrounds introduce very different perspectives into post-secondary and higher education as they interact with their peers, instructors, teachers, tutors, advisors and administrators. A measure of the competence of teachers and administrators is their awareness of diversity, their sensitivity to student differences in background, experiences and culture, and, ultimately, by how they make use of these demographic differences in the learning process.

The importance of match

This aspect of diversity also makes the ideas of student–institutional match and goodness of fit an important feature of retention. Think about the following four examples and their implications for retention:

- At the age of 40 a woman returns to higher education to complete a bachelor's degree that was interrupted some 16 years before. She wants to prepare for a post-graduate qualification. Her husband does not want her to complete her education, and her marital relationship is quite stormy as a result. Other adult or 'mature' students can relate to this situation, but teaching staff pay little attention to these personal experiences in either their advice or informal support, or in the class-room.

Implication: Is this a student who may drop out as she heeds the advice of her husband? Or will she persist in her educational work? Perhaps the marital relationship dissolves and the student finds herself in crisis. Will she then decide to leave higher education in order to address more immediate personal, family and financial issues?

- A student leaves a closely knit ethnic community that values the work ethic and the pursuit of gainful employment to attend a local college several times a week. The student's family and community stress that post-secondary education should lead to subsequent employment in a high-status profession. However, the student wants a career in the fine arts. He experiences considerable stress in trying to reconcile his family's values with his own, and he cannot access much help or understanding on campus.

  Implication: Who will help this student interpret his educational aims to his family and community? Will he withdraw from his involvement with his family and deal with any consequences that may jeopardize his status as a student? Will he feel alienation in the college because he cannot find a support system that helps him to value his choices?

- The first in her family to enrol on a post-graduate course, a young low-income student juggles employment with child-rearing responsibilities. By any measure, her stress level is very high, and she does not have the resources to obtain the mental health care she needs in order to manage this stress. The college mental health facility does not offer resources for her to obtain support from others experiencing a similar situation.

  Implication: Where will this student find the mental health care that she needs at this time in her life? Will the care she receives help her address the realities of single parenthood, work and college? Can the staff of her academic department help her handle or resolve these issues? Is it even their role to address these concerns?

- Adam learns best through multi-media presentations rich in visual display. He enjoys manipulating his environment and understanding the consequences of his action. His primary and secondary education was rich in media and electronic technologies that supported his acquisition of core educational competencies. He gets bored with more traditional teaching methods. The traditional lectures of the liberal arts course he is enrolled on are not a good method to support Adam's learning.

  Implication: Can the liberal arts college engage Adam in a manner that empowers and fosters his learning? Are the staff willing to integrate new teaching and instructional methods to engage Adam? Or will Adam decide that higher education is not for him and that he has to look elsewhere for the knowledge he seeks?

These examples reflect diversity and the role of demographics in defining the need for retention. In the first case, age and gender interact to create one situation, and in the next two cases ethnicity and income create different retention needs. Each example, however, demonstrates how important match or goodness of fit is to retention and the ultimate success of the student.

The diversity that each situation reflects creates different needs. The probability of a student discontinuing or even failing education lurks in these situations. A focus on retention must address a student's situation and what each one faces in the pursuit of educational aims. The demographics operating in each situation suggest that retention is far more than educational preparation, and far more than the mastery of educational competencies. Retention requires a psychosocial perspective, and it must address the personal and social needs that all students experience in their quest to achieve success in the educational situation of their choosing.

Diversity of students' educational careers

Educational careers are dynamic and will remain dynamic as we move away from traditional paradigms of post-secondary education and training. Students are adopting new methods in the manner in which they persist towards a degree, the courses they select to make them employable immediately and the manner in which they experiment with fields, professions and disciplines in order to identify their vocational, educational and career preferences. Some students may appear to be chaotic or undisciplined. Some students may appear to be confused or undirected or unfocused. But they may be negotiating their education in their own way, not bothering to adhere to the expectations of curriculum, pace and sequence their teachers and tutors try to dictate.

Financial pressures may require students to implement an employability strategy in which they take a package of courses (eg in information science) so that they can get an entry-level job as they continue to work toward a degree. Educational needs may suggest to students that they take local college courses in order to prepare for more rigourous study at university. Students with immediate employment objectives may take a very specialized course of technical training and then seek credit for this course as they move on in their education.

Consider this example. A young student, age 25, has been 'in and out' of a four-year college course over the past seven years. He has completed 60 per cent of the institution's graduation requirements by completing its courses and by transferring core requirements from a local college that offers lower-level educational opportunities. Tutors think that he is not persisting and lacks sincerity. However, coming from a family of modest means, the student has been alternating work and education. He is very sincere, obtains good grades and fears how his record will be interpreted by admissions officials when he applies for law school upon graduation at the age of 27.

The retention challenge for this student may be seen from a longitudinal perspective. The student is persisting but in a manner that is not consistent with more traditional notions of undergraduate education. How does the institution facilitate the success of such students over the course of the educational career they choose for themselves, which may extend over a long period of time? The student who moves in and out of active participation in education in order to earn money may obtain special supports to make this choice a successful one. Or the challenge may be met through helping the student to garner the resources to complete his or her educational objectives in six years rather than nine. Or the challenge can be met by helping the student navigate the transition from undergraduate to professional education.

Educational support takes on a new meaning in this approach to retention. It does not merely involve equipping students with core academic skills even though this is an important aspect of any retention programme. The ideas of goodness of fit and match have a role here. It is increasingly becoming important to know students from a personal perspective, and to understand their educational aims and aspirations in order to match a retention programme to their educational direction. *Retention is the process of helping students to meet their needs so they will persist in their education toward the achievement of the educational aims they value. Retention can achieve this through the mustering of supports that enable students to be successful, and the lowering or elimination of those factors that can disrupt the students' education, and that can ultimately result in their failure to achieve those educational aims they want.* Each institution must give some thought to the match between student needs and the supports the educational programme is willing to offer students. Post-secondary and higher educational institutions cannot ignore diversity in this regard. Diversity itself may suggest the needs of certain students or groups of students.

The diverse role education serves in the modern lifespan: lifelong learning and continuing professional development

Increasingly lifelong learning and education are becoming important to career relevance and success. The pace of career change in post-industrial market societies is tremendous, creating the need to upgrade core professional skills and to obtain knowledge, competencies and skills that allow for career mobility and ultimately career change. The turmoil and unpredictability of labour markets and corporate decisions require once-comfortable career professionals, managers and technicians to be wary of the 'one career, one employer' imperative that fitted previous generations so well. Career professionals who were once comfortable in their work situations may need to acquire new competencies to lead work groups, engage in research and development, and undertake new work roles, some of which did not even exist a few years ago. In this context, continuing, adult and professional education become more important for current workers than at any time in the past.

Retention here may come to mean not necessarily the acquisition of a degree but the completion of specific coursework, learning experiences or certificate course. The accountant who qualified 20 years ago may need to complete a certificate course in information systems management in order to oversee a new corporate financial network. An engineer may need to change from a manufacturing discipline to an environmental one while a social worker may require certification in geriatrics after years of practice in child welfare.

It is not and will not be unusual for professionals with degrees, post-graduate degrees and professional qualifications to seek out educational opportunities in technical schools, local colleges or post-secondary adult education courses. Many of these adult learners will be in career transition requiring specific and focused education for work and life roles that they now must execute with confidence and competence. Workers who find themselves with supervisory responsibilities, human resource professionals who need financial skills and technicians who require interpersonal skills come to these settings to obtain short-term education and training. Retention here means the completion of modularized education or a set of courses that prepare these students for the next steps in their lives and careers. Retention also means that students persist to gain the specific competencies they need now in their work lives and in their careers.

But education also fits into the lifespan of individuals in developing countries. New delivery systems for the teaching of literacy, core economic competencies and core academic skills may become part of a technical school's mission, which is as concerned with teaching the fundamentals as it is in granting two-year technical degrees. A particular technical school may sponsor an innovative curriculum supporting entrepreneurial skill development among people coping with poverty. The technical school awards a certificate that can in turn be transferred to a college or university. The certificate indicates that graduates fulfil requirements for core academic skills and core business competencies. Retention here means that the institution helps or enables those who enrol to complete the course and obtain the certificate.

Such training will become increasingly important over a person's lifespan. Someone working on his or her own entrepreneurial business venture may earn a focused and specific certificate. Another person may earn multiple modularized certificates, for example in car maintenance. A certificate for brake installation allows the student to obtain an immediate job while moving ahead to the next logical technical competence in the technical training and education course. The retention strategy may focus on the student's completion of enough certificates so that he or she eventually earns a two-year degree in the chosen technical area, which he or she has already worked in for some time.

In this situation, labour markets indicate viable directions to students, and training and educational curricula are flexible and adaptive enough to allow students a number of relevant options to choose from. However, the flexibility and adaptive capacities of curricula should not obscure the retention issues. Students can bring to the learning environment profound personal, social and cultural issues that can enhance, support and/or disrupt their persistence in the achievement of their educational aims. The essence of retention is to respond to these issues, so students can master the learning situation and proceed to fulfil those requirements that their educational aims dictate. The retention programmes and strategies of the future may need to be as flexible and adaptive as educational curricula.

THE PSYCHOSOCIAL NATURE OF RETENTION

So retention is not only a matter of finishing a degree. It is a matter of fulfilling students' educational aims that reflect their educational aspirations. Ultimately, these aims relate to students' lives and lifestyle, and how education fits into their life aspirations. It is the purpose of retention to assist students who require a support system to achieve their aims and achieve success in their roles as students.

What do we mean by 'the psychosocial nature' of retention? The phrase refers to the identification, assessment and resolution of those issues that can disrupt student success within an academic course if left unresolved or unfulfilled or if left to operate without change or modification. These issues operate within the person and within the environment. We conceive of the *environment of retention* as quite broad. It includes the environment formed by the academic setting inclusive of expectations, standards, performance requirements, resources and opportunities an institution offers. The environment of retention also extends beyond the formal course of study and/or the institution to encapsulate the grater community and the availability or lack of resources through the community including tangible resources like work, housing, recreation, health care and transportation, and intangible resources like encouragement, affirmation and emotional support. It also incorporates the student's peer group and family situation, and the broader cultural milieu within which the student functions in everyday life, which can frame, define and value education or various aspects of it, and career or life outcomes.

The individual student also is a source of issues. These can include aspirations and personal goals, expectations, values, commitments, and strengths and needs as they relate to the choice of an educational direction. The substantive needs of a student are not merely educational or academic in nature but also involve other factors like mental health, finances and the availability of social support.

The psychosocial nature of retention suggests five co-ordinating principles:

1. Retention involves the interaction of the students' environment, the post-secondary or higher education institution and the substantive needs of students. An educational institution that helps students fulfil or resolve the needs and issues they face will facilitate educational persistence and will be effective in the production of retention.

2. Retention involves the identification of issues operating in the environments of students outside the educational or academic situation as well as those operating within.

3. Each student must identify those issues that are most salient in his or her environment or personal situation that can reduce persistence in a particular educational course or situation. The more disruptive these issues become the more likely it is that the student will not persist.

4. The personal strengths and assets of students and the strengths and assets of their environments can offset the negative influence of the issues they face, and facilitate the persistence of students in the educational course or situation.

5. The students who are at most risk are those who face a considerable number of issues, who do not have a great deal of support in their personal and academic environments, and who do not receive strong support by the educational institution.

A STUDENT-CENTRED APPROACH TO RETENTION

These principles suggest that retention is a purposeful psychosocial intervention undertaken by a sponsoring academic or educational programme to reduce, weaken or eliminate those factors that can threaten persistence toward educational aims and aspirations, and to increase supports that will enable students to overcome the barriers they face. The basic aspects of retention as a psychosocial intervention form a helping process that is designed to support the individual success of students whose educational persistence and subsequent retention may be in jeopardy or at risk.

Student retention will continue to be an issue for a society and its educational institutions in flux. In other words, students experience first-hand this changing world, and it makes an impact on them in their quest to achieve their educational aims and aspirations. But retention cannot be merely programmed. Students face different issues and experience them in different ways. These issues and their experience by students have different consequences for educational persistence and retention.

This means that a student-centred approach to retention and the persistence students need to achieve retention are very personal matters. A student-centred approach means that retention is primarily for students and not necessarily for the benefit of the institution, although it can create many institutional benefits. A post-secondary or higher educational institution personalizes the retention process by:

● *Taking seriously the issues students face* and helping them to form relationships with caring staff who can assist them to identify, frame and subsequently resolve these issues. This means that any retention process requires an institutional commitment of staff who are willing to establish strong relationships with students.

- *Recognizing that retention is a decision process*. Some students may fade out of education. They face very real issues, are unsuccessful in addressing these issues and make decisions over time that weaken their involvement in education. Other students may face serious crises that push them out of educational involvement. A personalized approach to retention will reach out to students, help them to identify where they are at in the decision process and help them to resolve these decisions in a manner that is productive to them personally and educationally.

- *Offering a continuous programme of retention*. The institution recognizes that retention is a helping process that can exist over the lifespan of a student's career within an educational institution. Students can pick and choose their level of involvement in a retention effort. They should be able to phase out of the retention effort, and easily trigger a return if they feel there is a need. This means that students can go to a person seeking help when they have a setback, or when they face personal, educational or other issues that they feel they cannot handle on their own. They can then phase out of this encounter, but trigger involvement again if there is a need.

- *Framing retention as a helping process*. Ultimately, retention is a helping process in which relationship building is linked to individual strategies that the parties use to achieve a desired educational outcome. The key elements of the helping process are outlined in the box below.

---

1. Reaching out to students who have a need for retention support.
2. Forming strong, personal working relationships with these students that helps them to identify their aspirations and appraise their strengths and needs in the achievement of these aspirations.
3. Assessing what is going on, what strengths are operating, what issues are operating and what needs must be fulfilled.
4. Framing the retention objective and gaining commitment to it by both parties, as well as by key stakeholders in the educational and personal life of the student.
5. Identifying strategies and key action steps to achieve the retention objective and to produce an outcome; implementing and monitoring the retention strategies; modifying the strategies to ensure that students persist in their educational courses and realize retention, thereby enabling them to achieve their educational aims.
6. Involving key stakeholders in these action steps and strategies.
7. Taking action and revising strategies in the pursuit of the retention objective and outcome.
8. Achieving the objective, evaluating it and making key decisions about the continuation or redirection of the helping process.

---

9. Keeping the door open through follow-up, periodic contact and friendly visiting.
10. Assisting students to transition in their educational careers and endeavours.

CONCLUSION AND GUIDELINES

The sheer diversity of higher education today requires a student-centred approach to retention. New patterns of higher education and the social realities today's students face combine to demand more comprehensive approaches to retention rather than merely trying to keep students in higher education through narrow approaches to academic preparation and skill acquisition.

Contemporary retention efforts must go beyond an academic focus to address the personal, economic, cultural and career issues students face and must deal or cope with in order to be successful in higher education. The idea that students will enter higher education immediately after their secondary school education and persist for three or four years without interruption towards a degree no longer holds as the sole or primary approach to education. Educational institutions with an interest in retention must appreciate the diverse qualities of their actual and potential student bodies, and they must recognize the diverse aims students want education to fulfil.

In this chapter we have identified this diversity and illustrated how it can create the need for a dynamic retention effort and programme. We do not prescribe how an institution of higher or post-secondary education must respond to this diversity but we do highlight the importance of a student-centred approach.

Retention is indeed a very personal matter for a student, and it requires a flexible, comprehensive and supportive approach that fits well with a student's needs in order to make the retention effort or programme of an educational institution both viable and effective. We must also recognize another important aspect of a retention effort. Retention is a helping process that is geared to the needs of a particular student. The essence of retention lies in the ability to offer a student-centred helping process to each student with a desire or need for this kind of support. This student-centred helping process possesses the competence to deliver the five forms of support we identified in Chapter 1. Retention is a matter of matching the requisite forms of support to the needs of students. It involves offering students the emotional, informational, instrumental, material and/or identity support they require to master the academic expectations and requirements of the institution of higher or post-secondary education.

The educational institution's endorsement of and commitment to retention is vital to the success of any effort to keep students in higher education. The institution of higher or post-secondary education cannot merely pay lip service to the importance of retention. It requires a mission that highlights the importance of a student-centred approach to retaining students in higher education. The content of this mission is informed by the manner in which retention is practised (see the Introduction) and the student-centred qualities of retention (see Chapter 1).

Part II
The institutional framework of retention

Part I

3

The properties of the institutional retention mission

MAIN POINTS OF THE CHAPTER

- The institutional retention mission is composed of institutional, organizational and student-centred properties that work together to support the retention and persistence of students. These properties together indicate to the members of the educational community that retention is a priority.
- There are four properties of institutional commitment to retention: 1) the priority the institution places on retention; 2) the broad scope the institution assigns to retention; 3) the important role members of the academic community serve in any retention effort; and 4) the identification of the supports and resources the institution commits to retention.
- The organizational properties of the retention mission include: 1) broad endorsement of retention throughout the institution; 2) recognition and legitimization of the pervasiveness of retention roles and activities; 3) devolution of the retention mission.
- Student-centred properties of retention involve ease of use, the availability to students of personalized and dedicated relationships, and an outcome-orientation to retention and persistence.
- The institutional retention mission is strengthened when it is co-ordinated with the teaching and student life missions of the post-secondary or higher education courses of study.

We closed the previous chapter with an emphasis on retention as a student-centred process. We asserted that retention is ultimately for the benefit of students and is not undertaken to create benefits solely for the institution of post-secondary or higher education, yet this does not dismiss or otherwise reduce the responsibility of the institution for the advancement of retention as a priority, an objective, a process or an outcome. Given the important responsibility that the institution must assume in retention, and the challenge an institution faces in this area, the institutional mission becomes increasingly relevant to the advancement of retention.

By 'mission', we do not refer merely to the formal, written statement of purpose and intent of the institution. Too often institutions craft mission statements only to fail to act on them in a timely and consistent manner. In this chapter, mission is what institutional representatives articulate, verbalize, try to put into action on an ongoing basis and struggle to make happen. The mission of retention resides in the minds and hearts of those who form the core of the institution of post-secondary or higher education. It comes alive when these representatives talk about, use and debate it, and when they seek to revise it if it proves not to be relevant or fails to guide the members of the institution who commit themselves to it.

THE MISSION OF RETENTION SIGNIFIES INSTITUTIONAL COMMITMENT

The most important property of the institutional mission of retention is that it underscores what is important to the members of the educational community. Without a mission statement regarding retention, members of this community may feel that retention is indeed important, but they may be uncertain about whether it is a priority of the formal institution and its leadership. Sam, a newly minted PhD, who is now teaching for the first time in a local college, reflects with a more seasoned colleague about his initial teaching experience. His experience illustrates the problems that can arise when the institutional mission of retention fails to give direction to this aspect of the teaching role in higher education.

This is my first opportunity to teach after my PhD. I thought that I would be teaching only content relevant to my field, and I would confine my teaching to what I know best, rehabilitation theory and practice. I am shocked what students bring into my classroom. They face major social issues like health problems, serious reading problems and inadequate financial support. At the end of a class session, I have at least five students who need to meet with me to discuss personal issues that interfere with their course work. At first I thought they were only giving me the run-around or making excuses. But as I listened, I realized that they were facing serious, very serious, issues. And it is not just a limited few. The school does not deal with this kind of material, and I certainly have not found any importance assigned to addressing these kinds of student problems by the college.

This vignette emphasizes a number of the same issues that Chapter 2 covers, but they are now offered from the perspective of the member of staff. Sam is shocked and overwhelmed. He wants to be a good and effective teacher of rehabilitation practice in a technically driven training course designed to help students find entry-level employment in a variety of human services. Yet the students also bring human service issues into the classroom. Sam wants to understand his role, and the activities relevant to retention that he needs to incorporate into this role so he can be responsive to his students. The imaginary dialogue might go as follows.

Sam: So, David, you have been teaching for almost two decades. You teach in an urban setting in a traditional university. You probably don't see these kinds of issues in advanced undergraduate and post-graduate or professional education.

David: I don't know where you have been! I have been telling you about this for almost three years, but it probably doesn't sound real until you deal with it yourself in the classroom. I must say, however, that I can't escape these issues. The students bring them into counselling, into the classroom, into independent study and thesis work, into my e-mail and voice mail, and into all my informal interactions. This is the reality. In the past, education was a time to remove oneself from the harsh world and move into the solitude of the academy. This meant into a protected setting. Now, students juggle economic, family and educational realities. They can be in transition in terms of health, mental health and employment. I am an educator in the postmodern sense so I have to address these issues in relationship to how they influence the education and educational experience of students. There is something not only for my students to learn here but for me too. This is education for life, and for fitting education into the realities of life.

Sam: I don't find anything in my college that says that this is an important part of teaching. The administration speaks about retention, but it is narrowly defined, typically dealing with students who have educational development needs or some preparation to do before moving into a specific curriculum. Don't get me wrong, I want to help my students, I want to see them successful. But I am confused about how far I go.

David: I can't avoid retention. My university defines it as a principal aspect of our teaching mission. It is part of the teaching staff role, part of our service and part of our student development work. If we ignore it, perhaps we won't have any students, or those students who need some enhanced supports will fall by the wayside. But I didn't come into higher education to see such negative outcomes.

Sam: Maybe this is the difference. You know it is part of your role. I'm not sure whether it is part of mine.

Same wants to hear from the institution. As a dedicated, new teacher he is willing to address a range of issues. In fact, given the focus and substance of his curriculum in rehabilitation, he begins to frame his willingness to address these issues as part of his students' professional development in the human services. But he himself needs support. He needs an understanding of what retention means to his institution in terms of scope and how important it is to incorporate these activities into his role as a staff member. Most important is that he needs to understand and set his own expectations regarding retention.

The four properties of institutional commitment

In Sam's situation, the institutional mission of retention can help him to advance his own teaching practice and his own work in student development. He should also become aware that he is not alone in his quest to make this mission a part of teaching. The institutional mission can illustrate the commitment the institution makes to retention and the resources that are available to the members of the academic community to advance retention. Four properties of institutional commitment to retention stand out in this vignette. They are:

- *The priority the institution places on retention.* The institution must make this explicit formally and informally. It can do this through institutional publications, policy statements and institutional programmes linked to publicizing and rewarding outstanding and creative retention efforts by members of the academic community.
- *The scope of retention.* Members of the academic community must understand tacitly or explicitly those issues that fall within the scope of retention efforts. As indicated in Chapter 2, we do not restrict retention to educational issues and needs alone, but identify other potential disrupters that broaden the potential environment of retention.
- *The role of members of the academic community in retention.* The institutional commitment to retention also highlights what each member of the academic community can offer students who face retention issues. For Sam, this means he can gain an understanding of the nature of the student–staff relationship, and how members of the teaching staff can address retention through their various and diverse teaching roles.
- *The supports and resources available for retention.* Members of the academic community should understand that they are not alone. The institutional commitment to retention indicates what is available to students and to the people who help them in the way of specific programmes, student development services and crisis intervention resources.

THE ORGANIZATIONAL PROPERTIES OF THE RETENTION MISSION

The institution's promulgation of the retention mission can offer members of the academic community the beginnings of a common mindset and language for engaging in retention efforts. This mindset underscores retention as a priority, and as part of the job of a range of people within the educational setting. Indeed, the principal organizational properties of an institutional retention mission are a *broad endorsement* of retention, the *pervasiveness* of retention and the *devolution* of responsibility for the retention mission.

Broad endorsement of retention

The educational institution that works to disseminate fundamental beliefs about the importance of retention will begin to enjoy broad endorsement by a number of academic, administrative and student development staff. Members of the teaching staff begin to understand that they are fundamental to the retention mission, or they realize that they have been practising retention within their various teaching responsibilities, so that the mission normalizes and endorses these activities and their importance.

> When one large university disseminated its retention mission, a social science staff member realized how important her efforts in working with minority doctoral students had been over the previous 10 years. She was always willing to intercede into student crises, which typically related to financial needs, particularly for those doctoral students embarking on their dissertations. In the back of her mind was the research that illustrates how minority doctoral students can halt their education even at the point of the dissertation because they must address some pressing financial need. Her approach to retention is to advocate that students obtain research positions, jobs in the community or fellowships. She now believes that a broader and more formal endorsement of retention by the institution will strengthen her work to help doctoral students complete their dissertations. Increasingly, she finds her colleagues and other members of the academic community talking about retention, and how they can support students rather than seeing them fall by the wayside.

Recognition of the pervasiveness of retention roles and activities

A broad endorsement of retention can result in the ownership of the many responsibilities it involves by members of the academic community who in the past may have failed to perceive the important roles they serve in the achievement of retention outcomes. The educational institution cannot merely offer a specialized retention programme centralized in a certain part of its administration such as student counselling, although many institutions will have these specialized retention programmes. However, it is equally important to move retention efforts out of isolated academic enclaves and to integrate them into the roles of many different people who learn that retention is a fundamental aspect of the institution's mission and of their own work.

In a typical educational institution, there are many people who can add value to the retention mission. Members of the teaching staff can play an important role in any retention efforts at all levels of post-secondary and higher education. Personal tutors may come to realize that they are essential to 'personalizing' the educational experience of individuals and small groups. They are in the position of working closely with students and come to know their needs and strengths. Personal tutors are in a position to tailor on an individual basis the educational and personal supports specific students require in order to achieve their educational aims. Academic and career advisors can be as influential. They may understand students in a more personal way than can academics teaching in larger contexts like lecture halls and laboratories. These kinds of personal teaching and counselling roles may be the backbone of the institutional retention system. They can foster strong and enduring relationships that personalize the educational experience and prevent students from making decisions that result in dropping or fading out.

A good retention system also pervades the administration of the institution so that the programmatic scope of retention incorporates administrators at various levels including the course, department, college and university. These administrators can be the linchpins in the deployment of the retention mission and its translation into action within a specific area of the life of a college or university.

The retention mission can also extend into student life. Organized sports clubs, social clubs, professional associations, student unions, colleges, fraternities and sororities offer contexts and settings in which student leaders, advisors and alumni can become part of the retention effort.

Devolution of the retention mission

We alluded previously to the importance of moving the commitment of retention from centralized and upper levels of the educational institution into the actual roles of the members of the academic teaching staff and others who interact with students on a daily basis. This is another important organizational property of the retention mission. Without such devolution, areas of the academic community and administrative bureaucracy might fail to work together or to realize the importance of their contribution to retention as an objective of the educational institution.

Academic settings can be an amalgamation of different subcultures, and national situations do differ. Bureaucratic practices can interplay with entrepreneurial ones. The informal life of academic teaching and research exists alongside a strong business orientation to operations. Thus we are reluctant to prescribe how an institution should devolve the retention mission. The following example, however, shows how important it is to ensure that each academic unit translates the institutional retention mission into the life of the unit in a manner that makes sense to it but that nonetheless elevates the retention mission as a priority of the unit.

Devolving the retention mission: an illustrative example

A dean of a department of business studies works with the university's council of deans to frame the institutional retention mission. Once they have formulated the mission, the business studies dean announces that her work has just begun. She takes the mission back to her department and examines it very closely with all academic and administrative staff as well as with student representatives involved in the governance of the department. The dean's aim is to create an annual retention strategy for this academic unit.

The university's retention mission underpins this strategy. But the members of the academic unit go further to develop their own substantive strategy to address retention. They examine enrolment trends, and their student marketing efforts to colleges and universities. They analyse patterns of student persistence, and conduct an annual needs assessment of the issues students face in the completion of degree requirements and specific courses. The academic unit is able to identify those factors that can jeopardize the persistence of students. They initiate work to create new programmatic linkages like business mentorships early in a student's academic career, specialized counselling services and key educational skills development in areas like professional writing, business mathematics, and entrepreneurial and managerial problem-solving.

The strategy also incorporates educational activities that help academic, student development and administrative staff gain a strong sense of their own roles in the process of retention. These educational activities foster more dialogue, criticism and reflection. Ultimately, the staff of the department come to realize that retention is an integral part of their roles as teachers, advisors or administrators.

Broad endorsement, pervasiveness and devolution are three properties that can serve as the foundations of any organizational programme of retention since they will ensure that the institutional commitment to retention is real and that the academic community comes to value it. These properties also suggest that institutions of post-secondary and higher education should not rush into the creation of formalized retention programmes without first creating a strong sense of commitment to retention. Programmes involving the identification of at-risk students, the creation of specialized academic remedial programmes and the expansion of student counselling services are indeed important aspects of retention. But ultimately, for these programmes to be successful, the institution must increase awareness and build on the assets various academic and administrative staff bring naturally to retention.

Many members of the academic community have something to offer a retention effort. Typically, their most significant assets may simply be overlooked by the institution. These include the relationship staff members have with actual students, and the awareness the members develop of student needs through their constant interaction with the 'lived experience' of their students, an experience that often can be quite dramatic. This means that retention begins with individual students, and reinforces the importance of the student-centred properties of the retention mission.

THE STUDENT-CENTRED PROPERTIES OF RETENTION

The institutional mission of retention captures the spirit and substance of the student-centred approach to retention outlined at the end of Chapter 2. Retention is a psychosocial process in which the institution facilitates the provision of support and help to those students facing difficult barriers to persistence in and completion of their academic courses. Three properties of the institutional retention mission strengthen the student-centred approach to retention: 1) ease of use; 2) personalized and dedicated relationships; and 3) an outcome-orientation.

Ease of use

Retention within the context of post-secondary and higher education should offer students a set of services and supports that are easily triggered and easily used so that students can get what they need in a timely if not an immediate fashion. This attribute is not so simply achieved. It implies accessibility of the retention options available to students. The time constraints, multiple responsibilities and countervailing expectations that students face may need to be addressed by the institution through flexible time arrangements, the use of alternative communication technologies and the availability of geographically dispersed advice services.

Ease of use can also demand that retention options are sensitive to the cultural attachments of students as well as their emerging adult identities. A female student from a tightly knit Arab-American community may require a different kind of retention response from a female student from a Jewish-American community. Cultural sensitivity may be a key competence of an institution's retention mission if it is to facilitate ease of use in an educational environment increasingly characterized as diverse or multi-cultural.

Personalized and dedicated relationships

This second property that gives the institutional retention mission a student-centred character is relevant to those post-secondary and higher educational settings that are seeking to build strong connections between institutions and their students. Students are probably drawn to certain settings because of their courses, unique educational assets and scope of educational offerings, yet once these students arrive they can feel overwhelmed by the sheer anonymity of an institution that great size and complexity can create. Such qualities can dwarf students and make them feel that they are merely one of many. This is a dangerous situation from the perspective of retention. Students can easily disengage from the institution, or merely fade away, as they feel that they do not count or that no one really knows them.

This is when relationship formation becomes so important as a way of anchoring the student to the setting. It may be difficult for a large institution to help students to form individual relationships. Nevertheless, it may be an essential competency of the institution. Finding ways for each student to relate to someone is a job of everyone connected to the educational community. Some students will find these outlets on their own through membership of voluntary service groups, religious organizations or student associations. Other students will seek out members of the teaching staff, tutors or other academic staff and strike up relationships that may be characterized more by friendly visiting than by academic motivations.

But these examples rely on self-initiation and self-direction by students themselves. Those students who do not actively seek out such relationships may need them the most. Members of the teaching staff are important here. Expanded roles for staff that do not confine teaching solely to the classroom, laboratories or lecture halls can incorporate aspects that personalize the learning situation and foster the kinds of strong relationships that may be essential to the achievement of persistence and ultimately to retention. Members of staff who expand their roles into tutorials, independent studies and small group projects can be a pivotal strategy of the institutional retention mission. Students can get close to these members of staff and learn directly from them about their love for a subject matter, their commitment to an academic discipline and their understanding of a profession.

This exposure and the role modelling that is embedded within it can help students to formulate a personal vision of their own career direction and give meaning to their own academic experience. It is likely that students who have such strong relationships will turn to these people during times of stress, crisis or disruption when personal circumstances propel them to make critical decisions about their educational involvement and persistence. The relationship can go a long way to support students and help them to navigate uncertain periods in their educational careers. It is easy for students to leave a situation when they feel depersonalized. Strong relationships can go a long way to ensure that this state of affairs does not occur.

An outcome-orientation

Retention should result in outcomes that students value in relationship to their academic aspirations and aims. Framing the purpose of retention as degree completion overlooks the various realities that motivate students to seek out post-secondary or higher education. Some students will treat their educational experience as a period of experimentation with the outcome of choosing a direction. Their parents or significant others may dismiss this as 'Sam finding himself'. This is serious work and is certainly relevant to retention. Finding out about one's likes and dislikes, what one values, and personal strengths and limitations can serve an illuminative function for students. Based on this experimentation, students may choose to remain in education, try a different subject or select a new career direction. Other students may decide to leave higher education temporarily or permanently. The retention process can help students to sort this out so they experience a tangible outcome as a result of this stage of their lifespan. Decisions are critical ingredients of retention, and should be respected for all the diverse options they can open for students.

Other students will want to accomplish a substantive educational outcome. They are goal-directed or career-directed, and concerned about the substance and content of their education. Learning specific content, mastering knowledge and skills, and moving towards a degree in a timely fashion may be important to these students. Some students may fall short of their own expectations or they may perform poorly in some courses. They may want help to improve their basic educational competencies, gain advanced competencies within a specific discipline and take on increasingly difficult courses. Retention for these students may mean tailoring a developmental educational course to their needs, using testing to illuminate educational assets and needs, or devising a tutorial process that enables students to move on in their studies.

Some students will be disinterested in educational content for the sake of learning alone. They are eager to achieve a career outcome and will want to link their education to the world of work, subsequent or current employment, and career. Retention here may require the linkage of academics to the real world of work, profession and career. These students may want increasing exposure to the work world, and achieve this through volunteer activities, community service, traineeships, paid work experience, mentorships with practising professionals, and independent studies focusing on learning about aspects of certain professions.

The student-centred properties of retention imply that educators should not prescribe outcomes for students. This is up to the student and not the institution. We must confront a reality that looms large in the world of post-secondary and higher education. For many students higher education is a period of self-exploration, self-discovery and decision making even though the demands family, work and economics place on students do not make this period a leisurely or relaxed one. Retention is an outcome, and it can be quite diverse in substance and form. Ultimately, students need to come to grips with what they value, where they want to go and how they want to lead their lives.

CONCLUSION AND GUIDELINES

The retention mission of the educational institution should help teaching staff, other staff and students understand how the institution seeks to foster the success of its students. The key properties should foster awareness of the student-centred focus of retention.

The retention mission probably does not stand by itself independently of the other missions an educational institution must pursue. Certainly, the retention mission complements two other important missions of an institution of higher or post-secondary education: the institution's teaching mission; and the institution's student life mission.

The integration of the teaching and retention missions

An institution may have a teaching mission that incorporates diverse forms of teaching into it including:

- classroom- and seminar-based teaching;
- research projects;
- teaching, tutorial and instructional experience with undergraduate students;
- field and clinical instruction;
- laboratory-based research projects;
- community service instruction;
- independent, thesis and dissertation studies.

Within the context of these multiple forms of teaching and learning, its graduate mission statement might therefore be as follows:

> Through a diversity of learning opportunities, students can demonstrate their strengths, interests and capabilities, and refine these through various kinds of academic challenges that enable them to advance their knowledge, skills, attitudes and competencies within their chosen academic subject. Teaching and academic staff can foster the retention of students by assisting all students to identify those forms of learning that help them to be successful as students and as scholars in their chosen field of inquiry or subject.

The integration of the student life and retention missions

Most institutions recognize that undergraduate education is much more than formal instruction and encompasses opportunities to develop socially, culturally, physically, spiritually and ethically.

Hence, institutions may choose to integrate retention strategies with student life missions, involving the fostering of the development of the cultural community in the institution, with help available to assist students to form links with campus groups, and social or other activities that enable them to develop themselves outside the academic sphere. In articulating the relationship between the retention and student development missions, an academic leader might note:

Higher education is a period of self-discovery. But more and more students are working and more students are commuting than ever before. This means that we must be even more innovative to help students find a 'home' on campus that encompasses more than their academic career. Commitment to student development is in part opportunistic. If a student forms a good relationship with a member of staff, group leader or student leader, then we will be better able to identify the academic, personal or other issues that can prevent academic success. Students can benefit from a range of on-campus relationships, and these relationships form a key to retention.

4

The retention assets of institutions of higher education and their communities

MAIN POINTS OF THE CHAPTER

- When it comes to retention, we should not treat the institution as a singular community.
- Institutions of post-secondary and higher education and the communities that compose them possess a diversity of assets to support student retention and persistence. They offer a wellspring of resources.
- Diversity itself is the foundation of a good retention effort, and diversity is found in the communities that the educational institution or course helps develop particularly in relationship to fostering the educational access and participation of the members of these communities.
- For the purpose of retention, it is useful to differentiate three forms of community: 1) families and the intimate support systems of students; 2) groups formed by identity, ethnicity and other social attachments; and 3) communities and groups that emerge in the institution.
- Families can legitimize the aspirations of students, transmit to students strong values concerning education, offer stories to reinforce the commitment of students to education, and offer emotional sustenance, encouragement and tangible resources.
- External communities like service organizations, social service agencies, youth development schemes and ethnically based associations can transmit strong values regarding the importance of education, offer role models, open opportunity structures, mobilize resources to support access

to education, assist students to troubleshoot barriers and affirm the identity and aspirations of students.

- Assets of internal institutional communities like student government, student associations and student interest groups can offer career development, informal guidance regarding the formal curriculum, counselling, and recreational, cultural and leisure outlets.
- In making the institutional retention mission a reality, it is important for the post-secondary or higher education institution to link to its communities to form partnerships that target specific issues, students and resources. This can be done through collaborations with families, secondary schools and community organizations.

The institutional mission of retention underscores the importance of helping students to find their way, particularly when this can be most confusing and overwhelming for them. Retention underscores the institution's caring for its students, and the importance of building individualized and personalized relationships with students and bringing together resources that assist students to pursue their educational and career aims successfully. In this chapter we recognize the diversity of assets institutions of higher education possess that are relevant to their systems of retention. The institution and the communities that compose and relate to it are a wellspring of retention assets. Our aim in this chapter is to explore further the range of resources available to an institution in acting on its retention mission.

Some of these assets are obvious. They involve the core academic development programmes, advice and counselling opportunities, and career preparation opportunities that many institutions offer their students, particularly in the undergraduate and pre-professional years of education. Other obvious assets include accessible financial aid schemes, employment options, work-study and specialized programmes for students who are considered to need and/or deserve special supports. These assets are considered later in the chapter.

At this point, we want to suggest that diversity itself forms the underpinnings of a good and effective institutional retention effort. We cannot treat the institution of post-secondary or higher education as a singular, homogeneous community. It is a diversity of communities involving those communities that compose the institution and those communities that form reciprocal relationships or even partnerships with the institution. Educational institutions are diverse because the communities that form them are diverse. Students who form strong links with communities that strengthen their commitment to education, affirm their goals, direction and aspirations, and encourage them symbolically and instrumentally may create for themselves their own retention support system.

We differentiate in this chapter three different forms of community that constitute the retention assets of institutions of higher education or post-secondary training. First, there are the families of students. Second, there are those broader communities formed by identity, institutions and ethnicity. Third, there are those communities that emerge within the institution. Each of these communities can offer intangible and tangible resources to students. An educational institution can incorporate the assets of each of these communities into its retention systems and efforts.

THE ASSETS OF FAMILIES AND INTIMATE SUPPORT SYSTEMS

Most students do not come to higher education isolated from their own families and intimate support systems. Indeed, families themselves can be the impetus for students to engage or otherwise participate in post-secondary or higher education. Take, for example, the many students who enrol in higher education as the first in their families to do so. They come to the educational institution aware that they are the first to move on to higher education, and they are aware of the high expectations for their performance. A good number of these students will have in mind the 'stories' that frame their involvement. These stories can be about relatives, friends of the family or esteemed people who have been successful in the professions, business and other walks of life. Some students do very well with these expectations. They readily translate them into their own aspirations and form a strong sense of educational identity based on the encouragement and support of their families.

Other students may come with less developed ideas of what they want to achieve through their education. Nonetheless, their families stand as important support systems in their lives and can stress to the students the importance of persevering. These families can encourage students to explore academic and career options, and help them keep in mind that the educational process is a personal journey in which participation itself can lead to clarification of aspirations and the translation of these aspirations into educational and career goals. In fact, families may serve as a student's anchor in the initial period of higher education when the student may become demoralized or disaffected, and at a practical level, a retention programme can create partnerships with families with the aim of enlisting their successful support of their members in the mastery of the role of student.

Some educators will argue that this is above and beyond the mission of post-secondary and higher education. College is a time for autonomy, gained through emancipation from family and parents. It is time for independence and a time for self-sufficiency. Perhaps this is so, if indeed these are the values of the student and the student's family. But students will probably stay involved with their families for some time and look to their families for support when they are uncertain, under considerable stress or indecisive.

61

Family is not necessarily something the student must escape, but a social structure that can be instrumental in helping students to navigate the journey of higher education. Many students remain at home, work – sometimes full-time, commute to university, and depending on their culture, may maintain strong ties to family identity, traditions and rituals. If students have these resources then it may be possible to mobilize them in the name of retention. If students recognize the importance of their families, why not involve them? The choice is up to the student. Autonomy, independence, self-sufficiency and emancipation are all values that may or may not be important to the success of an institution's students. What is important is that these students have opportunities to achieve their dreams and their aspirations, ones they may share with the members of their families. A US university institute which draws many of its students from the local Mexican community operates a retention programme according to four principles:

1. Know your students and their situations.
2. Understand the role of family in the lives of students.
3. Work with students in the institution and in the context of their families, if students desire this and find it acceptable.
4. Reach out to families and involve them in the educational life of students. They can offer much to the aim of educational persistence and retention.

Perhaps some readers will find this family outreach programme too idyllic, as many students can be alienated from their families, on their own or unable for various reasons to count on any family support, let alone family involvement. Some students themselves may report that their families are not supportive of their careers in higher education. Former Surgeon General of the United States, Dr Koop, asserted that 'family is function not necessarily structure'. He was suggesting that some people might invent the postmodern family, creating their own support systems through friendships, self-help alliances, room-mates and intimate relationships. Educators often see functional families form among students who create bonds among themselves in professional or academic courses. Friendships and intimate relationships can blossom within study groups, group projects and classrooms as students share experiences and grow to know one another and lend support. These relationships can create their own stresses, but they can also help students find tangible support and assistance.

Few students are without a support system or a reference group to guide them in their pursuits, show or demonstrate encouragement, or offer help during challenging times during which the decision to quit education is seen by the student as the sole option. Those with an interest in retention will not want to ignore these support systems. As a consequence, they may want to extend their frame of reference to include an understanding of how family, extended family, friendship circles and intimate support systems influence retention. These structures and what they can offer students certainly should be incorporated into what we describe in Chapter 2 as the *environment of retention*.

THE ASSETS OF EXTERNAL COMMUNITIES

We can broaden the resources available to retention beyond the families and intimate support systems of students. Communities that mediate between the institution of post-secondary and higher education and students are also instrumental in the process and outcome of retention. Community structures that mediate between higher education and students can take several different forms. In some communities, these mediating structures involve religious institutions and churches, and concerned religious or spiritual leaders; in other communities they can involve businesses and business leaders; while in others they can include service organizations, social service agencies, ethnic-based associations, youth development organizations or projects, and advocacy and support groups.

There is a diversity of these structures in any given community, but they may serve the same functions when it comes to the participation of students in higher education, the persistence of students and the subsequent retention of students. The core functions they share in common consist of:

- the transmission of values regarding the importance of post-secondary training and higher education;
- the opening of opportunity structures for students who may not otherwise obtain entry into post-secondary training and higher education;
- the mobilization of resources to support entry to and involvement in post-secondary training and higher education;
- troubleshooting barriers to persistence and retention, and the sustenance of students during challenging times that could result in the discontinuation of education if not addressed;
- the affirmation of identity that legitimizes involvement and success in post-secondary education and training, and in higher education.

Transmitting the value of education

This may be one of the most important functions mediating structures can offer. Take, for example, a group of young first generation Chaldean students who are making decisions about entry into post-secondary or higher education. These students are the first of their community group to enter higher education. When their parents immigrated, they founded small businesses that became essential to the livelihoods of their families and communities. They have strong aspirations for their children's education, and their advancement through education or training. The children gather at their local church, which serves as the centre of their community. Organized religion is particularly important in this community, and two universities have co-sponsored an 'education day' in co-operation with the church to increase awareness of higher education options. The religious leaders attend, thereby affirming the importance of education and conveying symbolically the importance of the educational success of the community's youth. The church serves as the focal point for this event, and local business leaders as well as professionals participate in it. This underscores the importance of higher education to the children, who are aware that the leaders of their community have come to endorse symbolically and ceremoniously their educational futures.

There is every reason to believe, as this example illustrates, that retention can and should start at the time that young people begin to frame post-secondary training and higher education as an option that is important to them.

Linking together recruitment, persistence and retention makes sense within the context of any outreach effort on the part of an institution of post-secondary or higher education. 'Valuing of education' can come early, and it certainly can involve the greater community from which students come in order to establish this effort as an important and legitimate one.

Opening opportunity structures and mobilizing resources to support entry and involvement in higher education

Higher education represents an opportunity structure essential to the advancement and mobility of people in either developing, industrial or post-industrial economies. In the United States, the demise of affirmative action is resulting in a precipitous drop in the enrolment of students from minority groups in undergraduate, post-graduate and professional education. In the US context and beyond, viable mediating structures within communities that help link students to higher education and make educational options available to students are critical more than ever, as people of minority status find that traditional opportunity structures are closed to them.

Increasingly in the US and elsewhere social service organizations an agencies recognize the importance of assisting people coping with poverty, disability or other social situations to take advantage of higher education. These agencies recognize higher education as a personal asset, and understand that the people whom they seek to help to take advantage of this education may not be seen as viable or desirable candidates by institutions of higher education. Specialized programmes can be developed to support the involvement in higher education of people coping with such problems, and help them to make choices about future education and career alternatives, fulfil educational needs and satisfy essential prerequisites in order to gain admission to higher education. Without these supports, individuals may fail to compete in the environment of higher education. With these supports, people can assemble a portfolio of accomplishments that begins to open up new educational and career opportunities.

These options may be based in adult education settings, technical schools or community colleges, but they all share a common commitment to help people who experience prejudicial treatment or bureaucratic obstructions to gain opportunities they otherwise would not have available to them. They are designed to open educational options as a fundamental opportunity structure.

Troubleshooting barriers to persistence and retention

Some mediating structures will stay in the background until there is a student need that they can address through, for example, the provision of tangible resources like emergency loans, scholarships so that students can continue their education without interruption, mentoring relationships or paid work-study opportunities. Alumni organizations, charitable organizations or associations, and local professional associations are examples of mediating structures that can fill important roles and/or gaps in any retention effort.

A commitment to persistence and retention of students must recognize that the educational career is not without barriers, impasses or serious life events that can disrupt involvement and participation. Students may need access to assistance that may not be readily available through institutional channels owing to the time of the year, bureaucratic requirements or availability. Community organizations may be able to offer the required support with little notice.

Accessible and available cash may be an important contribution of these kinds of mediating structures. But this is not the only contribution such groups can make to the encouragement of student persistence and retention. Institutions may develop active relationships with related or local professionals or technical associations. One US community college collaborates with five technical associations to offer a mentoring programme that exposes students to the 'real world of the profession' through active involvement with practising graduates. These mentors help students understand the particular technical branch of computer science they have chosen to study. The mentors meet at the work site to explain projects, help students identify the technical skills involved in the project and explore aspects of the work setting students find satisfying and dissatisfying. The associations also sponsor a work-study programme that is available to students who are trying to make career decisions in the application of computer and information science.

The associations do not reserve these programmes for the most promising students. They want to support students who may need to augment their vocational maturity, to explore their decisions and to understand where their academic decisions can lead them. They want to foster a positive climate for decision making that can help students to sort out their own personal interests and commitments thereby reducing these as potential frustrations that can lead to academic discontinuation.

These associations have committed themselves to service and want to maintain a strong working alliance with colleges on behalf of students. Indeed, whether the associations engage in loans, scholarships, mentorships or work-study programmes, they have a strong interest in serving as a student-centred resource.

They can make an important contribution to sustaining students during periods when students require accessible support.

Affirming identity

Some mediating structures will themselves help students to form 'communities of identity' that help them to reduce the depersonalization that large, bureaucratic institutions can engender. These mediating structures can foster alternative support systems for students who see themselves as possessing or developing identities that may be at odds with the social definitions commonly endorsed as correct or acceptable. These mediating structures may also be instrumental in protecting students from hostile or abusive treatment by members of other groups. These identities can be formed and shaped by ethnicity, gender, sexual orientation and disability. Students may find acceptance from these groups that helps them to understand how they want to function, what roles they want to assume and how they want to proceed with their careers. Some students may find a convergence between their social identities and their career interests, and may use their college experiences as conduits for the exploration of these identities through assignments, projects, papers and presentations.

Students forming and developing their social identities may be at risk of discontinuing their educational careers. It may be difficult for them to find role models with whom they can identify and with whom they can form the relationships they need in order to frame and interpret their own experiences and choices. Peers or staff in the institution may undermine, either intentionally or unintentionally, the identities of these students, and they may become alienated.

Student support groups

Retention for students who are forming a sense of self based on social identities and social commitments may benefit through membership of specific groups that support them, their choices and their identities. These groups can offer a sense of community formed by a network of supportive relationships that help students to define who they are and where they want to go in their lives and careers. These networks can expose students to self-help and mutual support activities as well as to role models. Such groups may also form their own institutions – agencies and organizations – that offer outreach, tangible assistance, education and support to their members. The involvement of students in these activities can create meaningful educational events helping students to shape their sense of career:

Betsy came to law school firmly rooted in her identity as a lesbian. She was quiet about her sexual orientation but nonetheless she was certain about the life commitments and choices she had made. What puzzled her was how to become more active in her community, and how to link her identity and her career. She came to law school to discover how to serve as a lawyer active in the lesbian movement. She did not know whether she would last in the school, as it was known for its male-dominated heterosexism. She was surprised when a male member of staff introduced her to a community-based legal advocacy group devoted to fostering the rights of gay, lesbian and bisexual individuals. She found a home there. The member of staff helped her to undertake several clinical law projects, and the members of the group helped her to see several different career paths. Although there was not an active group in the law school, Betsy felt that her connection to the community cemented her commitment to law.

The importance of university–community partnerships

These functions demonstrate that retention is not merely undertaken through the organization of academic activities. Consistent with our approach to retention, that is, as a psychosocial intervention, the idea of helping students to remain within post-secondary and higher education does require the identification of how the community outside the institution can support retention aims and outcomes. A 'good' retention effort not only recognizes the importance of these external community assets, but it helps all students to define their own links to the community. A good retention effort encourages each student to take advantage of the community networks the institution creates within the larger community in which it operates. The idea of a network takes the full burden of retention away from the student and the institution, and reframes the responsibility for retention as a student–institution–community partnership.

The linkage of the institution of higher education to these external communities also highlights the importance of proactivity to retention. The retention effort should not concentrate all its strategies in remedial or even crisis activities, even though these are important to a fully developed retention programme. The message in this section is that retention needs to be proactive and it must be initiated as early as possible, perhaps even linked to marketing and student recruitment. And it is developmental in nature. A good retention programme reaches out into communities to those mediating structures that can influence and foster the development of potential students.

School partnerships

One of the most fundamental of these partnerships lies in the relationship between institutions of higher education and secondary school-level education. These partnerships capture the three important qualities of retention identified in the previous paragraph. They encourage retention to be initiated early, proactive and developmental. Those institutions of higher education that initiate partnerships with secondary schools are building awareness of higher education as an opportunity at an early age, and they help the staff, school students and families involved in these schools to begin to contemplate the importance of higher education. They also help school students and families to begin to develop a long-range plan that supports subsequent involvement in higher education.

There is a range of innovative practices these partnerships can support. One important practice may simply lie in helping school students and their families to experience the campuses of potential places of higher education study. Such a practice can demystify higher education for young students and families, and help them to understand the many opportunities, activities and resources available in contemporary institutions of post-secondary and higher education. Other practices can include:

- the involvement of the teaching staff of higher education in primary and secondary school education;
- the collaboration among teachers of primary, secondary and post-secondary education in developing core educational competencies, the achievement of which will enhance success in higher education;
- the formation of educational consortia among schools at all levels that focus the attention of educators on the importance of preparing students for success in post-secondary education in whatever form this takes.

In some communities, particularly those experiencing social distress or social change, the consortia may also include partners from local charitable, public and private organizations. Some of these partners will bring to the consortia the ability to organize learning opportunities focusing on basic educational, linguistic and cultural skills. Institutions like libraries, career development centres, youth clubs and community centres are examples of partners that universities may overlook in the development of their retention efforts.

Other partners will bring to the consortia the ability to organize work-related opportunities and experiences, for example local employers, large corporations, and employment and rehabilitation centres. Other partners can bring to the consortia health, mental health and social services that can support the principal mission of fostering retention.

Suffice it to say, a partnership can be of whatever scope is needed in order to achieve the aims of the retention effort. Institutions of higher education, however, will have to define the role these various community entities can serve in retention. Ignoring them, or failing to incorporate them, may limit the effectiveness of retention.

THE ASSETS OF THE INTERNAL INSTITUTIONAL COMMUNITY

We should not limit the idea of retention assets to the external community alone. Many institutions of post-secondary and higher education possess a range of informal and formal assets that they integrate into student and academic life. A retention effort can incorporate these assets into its service matrix as a way of expanding retention and persistence strategies. We explore these internal assets as they pertain to student organizations, and the opportunities for student development available in the institution.

Student government and student interest groups

Student government is a critical asset to any retention effort, particularly if the structure of student government and the groups and associations it encourages reflect the diversity of the student body. Diversity as a quality enhances student government as an asset because it will make available more supportive opportunities for students, more opportunities for students to strengthen their identities and more opportunities for students to match their preferences with a reference or activity group. Betsy's situation, described above, is illustrative here. Betsy wanted to integrate her professional aspirations, advocacy commitments and sexual orientation, but could not find an interest group in the institution that reflected her values, interests and concerns. The law school did not legitimize her commitment to the advancement of gay rights, and the student associations within the law school did not offer such an interest group or see any reason to make one available. Fortunately, Betsy found an external group that affirmed her identity. Without this affirmation, Betsy might have discontinued her legal education.

A diverse structure of student interest groups and the capacity to foster diverse voices of students can help to focus retention efforts on the needs of particular subgroups of students. Indeed, this kind of diversity can make institutions of postsecondary and higher education more sensitive to the psychosocial, cultural, career and educational needs of their various students and to the groups that support them. Some practical assets form through such diversity. Students from any ethnic group may form an effort to reach out to newcomers to the institution. They form a system that offers each new student a dedicated relationship with another, more experienced, student. The system personalizes the educational experience, offers new students a relationship with someone who can help interpret their experiences in higher education and supplies one-to-one problem solving when it is needed. This dovetails into group activities that support socialization and cultural activities.

Groups may also emerge based on the diversity of the student body, and based on the encouragement they receive from the institution. Students may be attracted to these groups because they are relevant to the issues students experience, their emerging identities, or their political and cultural identities. On the face of it, a commitment to diversity may be seen as fragmenting the student body and reducing its ability to mobilize support for all students. However, from our experience and perspective, this diversity leads to a student body that truly functions as a federation. It fosters the values of being different as people yet unified as a student body that advances the interests of all students. Take, for example, a group of gay students who are committed to the advancement of the arts. This group actively organizes to include as many students in the humanities and fine arts as possible who want to 'know about the gay experience', and the group's meetings and events serve as a gathering place for practising artists who want to advance their craft. The group sponsors annual showings and competitions that offer members opportunities to show their work and have it critically appraised. A representative from the group serves in student government, and a staff member from the fine arts school advises the group, and advocates for its mission within the greater university community. A wide variety of other groups operate in a similar fashion.

These groups can link with more mainstream interest groups that foster the technical, cultural and social life of the institution and that help students connect their substantive career interests to the institution's support systems. Thus, several different student cultural groups organized around ethnicity may link together under the cultural arts umbrella of student government. Institutions can recognize through this kind of federation the importance of diversity and the importance of unity.

Students will decide individually whether they want to get involved in such groups as well as their level of involvement. Students vary in terms of their interests, commitments and the availability of their own resources. Involvement will vary by the nature of institutions and their ecology. An example is the authors' own institution, a large, urban research campus, where the 'typical' student works in the community, supports a family and has demanding financial responsibilities. Students may decide not to be active because of these responsibilities and the personal demands they create. However, other students will be involved.

What is important is that these groups exist, that they function well and that they are involved in shaping and advancing the retention mission of the institution. The groups offer a number of functions that are similar to the five we identified above for external community groups. They can:

1. reinforce strong values regarding the importance of post-secondary training and higher education;
2. foster opportunities for students;
3. mobilize resources to support continued involvement in higher education;
4. troubleshoot barriers to persistence and retention;
5. link the identity of students to educational careers.

However, unlike many community groups, these groups have a presence in the institution. One of their most important functions is to reach out to students in order to create enduring relationships or to offer opportunities for educational and cultural enrichment, networking among students and mutual support. They send a message to students, staff and administrators of the importance of having connections and experiences in the institution that help in the achievement of educational aspirations.

Higher education is more than requirements and formal course work

The role of diverse student groups in the institution suggests that higher education is more than what the institution requires of students in order to graduate. The modern institution of post-secondary or higher education is a hive of academic, scholarly and developmental opportunities. Retention does not mean merely persistence in formal education but also the potential involvement of students in the 'hidden curriculum' of higher education. The traditional student of the past is no longer the typical student. Students have demanding and busy lives, and there are numerous personal and social forces that can pull students away from the achievement of their academic aspirations. However, the institution has an important role in helping students to realize what is at stake, and in offering them the linkages, relationships and opportunities to help them to persist.

In considering the assets of the institution's community or even the cybernetic community of higher education, it is critical to understand the important role of relationships between students and representatives of the academic life of the institution. These relationships may be one of the most fundamental assets of a retention programme. They often emerge informally as students and staff realize that their interests coincide, or as staff members reach out to students in teaching a subject, field or profession. Retention may hinge on a student forming an enduring relationship with a staff member, academic counsellor or specific department that supports and nurtures the student intellectually, culturally and socially. These relationships may expand into research projects, personal tutorials, directed and independent studies, and special projects. For example:

The Midwest Urban Development Expedition, sponsored by a small four-year liberal arts college, brings students together from geography, biology, sociology, graphic art, computer science, history and literature to learn about the life of cities and how to understand them culturally. The interdisciplinary staff sponsored expeditions to major urban areas of Canada to conduct inquiries into the cultural life of big cities. The expedition required course work, attendance at several presentations and workshops, and individual consultation with tutors. Small interdisciplinary groups of students then conducted their fieldwork. Dissemination of findings often took the form of social gatherings of staff, administrators, students and interested professionals to learn about the findings and insights of the expedition teams. The project served as a strategy of integrating students and staff, and of building bridges between course work and career development.

Most students will come to realize that higher education is not secondary education. Although they must perform at an acceptable level in their academic courses, as they persist they may find increasingly higher levels of freedom in choosing their interests, relating to staff and pursuing their own substantive forms of education.

Academic curricula are changing as we write. Technical, liberal arts, scientific and professional forms of education at undergraduate and post-graduate levels are introducing service education, community projects, co-operative education and a variety of work-study options. Some institutions are experimenting with portfolios while others help students to target their learning requirements based on an assessment of the knowledge, skills and competencies they have garnered through previous work, training and life experiences.

These varied assets suggest a larger one. Students need, and should have available to them, opportunities to choose an academic direction, contemplate their choices and explore them. Students with an absolute understanding of the directions their lives will take are a minority. One reason that students may not persist in their education is that they do not have opportunities to develop a maturity that comes from the exploration of educational and career options that may be of interest to them. Increasingly institutions of higher education may need to assist students to undertake this kind of exploration and to link early academic experiences to the aim of expanding students' own sense of educational and career self-concept. This truly would be an institutional asset in service to the development of the individual student.

CONCLUSION AND GUIDELINES

There are tremendous assets supporting retention efforts both within and outside institutions of higher and post-secondary education. Institutional representatives with an interest in retention need only look around their institution and the greater community surrounding it to identify retention assets. A great many people have a strong interest in higher education since they understand that educational attainment and achievement may be one of the most important assets a person can acquire in a lifetime. As this chapter emphasizes, many people can relate to a student's quest for education, and family members and relatives, community professionals, religious and spiritual advisors, and professionals in social and community service agencies stand ready to assist colleges, schools and universities with their retention efforts.

It is unfortunate if an institution of post-secondary or higher education frames retention as an effort that requires only academic staff. As this chapter highlights, the allies of retention occupy many different niches of the external and academic community. However, to incorporate these assets into a retention effort, the educational institution must engage in community development. This means that the institution has to work systematically to:

- identify the internal and external stakeholders with an interest in and perhaps commitment to retention;

- reach out to these stakeholders and involve them in the development and improvement of retention efforts;
- develop roles for them so that they can contribute something of value to the retention effort;
- recognize and reward their involvement in order to strengthen their bonds to the retention programme the institution sponsors;
- keep them informed about the results and consequences of their retention efforts.

5

The infrastructure of retention and student support

MAIN POINTS OF THE CHAPTER

- The infrastructure of student retention and persistence forms the foundation supporting the extension and elaboration of other institutional retention efforts.
- In this chapter, we identify four functional areas forming the infrastructure of retention. These are awareness building, accessibility services, performance-based supports and transition services.
- Awareness building can occur at any point of the student's educational experience. Some awareness building efforts concentrate at the beginning of the experience, and often come in the form of orientation, while others facilitate the transition of students through their educational career.
- Good orientations help students to become aware of the relationships they need to be successful as students, how they can master the student role and how to link to the resources they require or may need in the future.
- Awareness building interprets the educational institution to the student, and the student gains insight into how the course of study works as a result of increased awareness of the institution.
- Accessibility involves helping students to get those accommodations they need to be successful as students. These accommodations often involve the organization of relevant resources, and the reduction of barriers so students can be successful in their role as students.

- Staff members are critical to making learning experiences accessible to students, and in formulating the accommodations students need to be successful.
- Individualized student support plans help students to identify and assess their performance issues, and to get the services and supports that help them to perform academically.
- Institutions need to recognize that performance issues not only arise early in the career of students, but can also emerge during the course of students' education including transition to higher courses, performance in major subject areas and fulfilment of requirements that are not in a student's area of academic strength.
- Sensitivity to major transitions in the career of students can help them to master each step in the educational process. These transitions may be academic in nature, career- or work-oriented, family- or relationship-oriented, and identity-oriented.
- The development of the institutional model of retention brings together the four functions of retention (awareness, accessibility, performance and transition) with critical interactions students can have with courses, staff, their peers and members of their communities.

Increasingly institutions of higher or post-secondary education offer an array of retention programmes and opportunities. These offerings are based on the idea that certain students need special attention as they move into new roles as students of higher or post-secondary education. Often the programmes kick in after these students experience problems with adjustment or performance. Others are more anticipatory; they come into play at crucial points in the careers of students to guide them through major decisions about their academic direction.

Some students will come unprepared for higher education. The purpose of an institution's retention effort is to help them become more prepared with special attention and special supports. Other students will come prepared, but will experience sometimes intractable problems as they move through their education. They require some kind of support system to overcome their problems, perhaps in addressing their academic performance in a required area of the curriculum or in addressing personal concerns that can disrupt their education if not resolved in a timely manner.

To appreciate the current retention efforts of institutions of higher or post-secondary education, we examined a range of institutional Web sites. This revealed a plethora of offerings, opportunities and course structures designed to keep students in higher education. In this chapter, we describe and document these offerings. We refer to them as the 'infrastructure of retention' because these programmes taken collectively not only reflect a broad commitment of many educational institutions to keeping students in higher education, but also form the basic foundation on which institutions build, extend or elaborate other retention efforts.

The box below gives a snapshot of this array of retention offerings, opportunities and programmes. These findings can be organized into four functional areas: awareness building, accessibility services, performance-based supports and transition services. These taken individually or together can represent what an institution of higher or post-secondary education means by retention.

EXAMPLES OF RETENTION EFFORTS AND SERVICES THAT INSTITUTIONS OF HIGHER EDUCATION OFFER TO THEIR STUDENTS

Awareness building efforts

- Information sessions on how the university or college operates.
- Orientations to student life and campus life.
- Orientations to academic work and expectations.
- Educational opportunities regarding safety and violence prevention.
- Student networking sessions.
- Orientation to subjects, professional courses and educational options within complex institutions.

Accessibility services

- Specialized supports to students with disabilities.
- Enhanced learning opportunities for students who need academic development.
- Modifications to the physical or learning environment to facilitate student participation.
- Financial arrangements and loan schemes.
- Enhancements to communication and other supportive technologies.
- Diversification of ways students can demonstrate their learning.
- Flexible housing arrangements.
- Modification of class schedules and innovations in scheduling and packaging courses and academic requirements.
- Staff involvement in linking students to academic opportunities and resources.

Services to support student performance

- Summer and inter-session enrichment opportunities.

- Individualized education plans.
- Mentoring in substantive academic areas.
- Peer tutorials and mutual support and problem-solving activities among students.
- Conflict-resolution activities and ombudsman services.
- Specialized academic courses of study for students with learning challenges.

Services to foster student transition

- Expedited updating of student records to facilitate the transfer of credits.
- Intensive preparatory programmes to facilitate transition to higher-level education.
- Helping students who are new parents to address role demands.
- Facilitating the integration of students into campus life.
- Career development and exploration services.

FACILITATING STUDENT AWARENESS

These offerings, opportunities and programmes help students to become aware of the educational institution, how it operates and the various resources available and to give students a basic understanding of how to take advantage of opportunities. These efforts are based on the idea that 'informed students are successful students' and that part of readiness is to be knowledgeable about the institution and its life.

Awareness building may start with informing potential students, for example, through courses that bring students to the institution for summer educational and preparatory experiences. Awareness building may start at the beginning of the education of a new cohort of students and continue throughout the early period of the students' educational experience.

In addition to offering students basic information, awareness building efforts may also incorporate several other retention objectives like reducing the anxiety of students, facilitating networking among students, linking students to advice services and career development, and helping students to form initial friendships or partnerships with their peers.

Orientations

A principal vehicle of awareness building is student orientation or familiarization. Orientations are often the first opportunity for staff to make an impression on students. Orientations often occur at some kind of transition time for students, when they may have mixed feelings about their participation in higher or post-secondary education. They may feel excited about getting started and filled with anticipation. They may also feel considerable anxiety that they are not up to the expectations created by their new roles.

Some students will be new to the university or college, coming directly from secondary education or adult education. Some students may enter after a gap between secondary education and higher or post-secondary education. Some students may already be enrolled in an institution, but moving into a different area of study, or into a pre-professional or professional course of study.

It is critical for educators to remember that orientations are for students, and not necessarily for the institution. It is important to base the design and content of the orientation on what students need, particularly what they need in order to make a good transition to a new educational experience. Many students may base their expectations on their most immediate or prior educational experience, and the orientation may be the first opportunity the institution and its staff have to help students reframe their expectations, attitudes and feelings about the next step of their educational journey.

From our own experience as educators, we find that the orientation is often a time for students to appraise the course of study they have chosen. They have an opportunity to meet with members of staff and to form initial relationships with real people. Many students want to know about whom to contact if they should experience problems or concerns in their course. They want to know how they will interact with members of the teaching staff, and assess whether their teachers are truly approachable. It is not unusual for students to be intimidated by staff initially. After all, many staff members are accomplished individuals, who have mastered the material and roles their students seek to master. The personalization of the orientation, that is, the degree to which the orientation helps students to become comfortable with and aware of their course of study and the people who compose it, is an important quality of awareness building.

Orientations offer opportunities for students to learn about one another, and to form initial impressions and relationships. One undergraduate course in health care administration bases its entire curriculum on student teamwork. The curriculum incorporates group projects and team formation at all stages. The course culminates in the completion of a major group project in health care by teams of students who work together intensively during their last term. The culture of teamwork is kicked off during the course's annual orientation by teams who graduated the previous year presenting their projects in the form of workshops to new, incoming students. The orientation then helps students to learn about the backgrounds and perspectives of their peers in anticipation that the first term will bring these students together into classroom-based work teams. Exercises helping new students to learn about one another link to exercises enabling students to learn about staff and how teachers can offer substantive resources to student teams. By the end of the orientation, students have transformed their expectations from working as isolated and individual students to working as team members who will be learning to advance health care.

Other less structured orientations often incorporate a component that encourages students to learn from one another. In these situations, more experienced students serve as orientation mentors to their incoming peers, enabling the new students to find out about departmental, course or institution policies and politics. The new students will learn about the staff, the best places to study, the restaurants that serve inexpensive but good meals, and how to obtain access to the resources of the institution including emergency funds, computer and Internet services, and textbooks. An orientation can influence how comfortable students will become at a particular educational institution, and can facilitate student mastery during the early periods of their educational experience.

Awareness building at other stages of the educational career

Awareness building can become important at other junctures of an educational career. Take for example the period that institutions devote to registration. Many institutions are increasingly automated in the delivery of registration services, and students may be able to effect registration through Web-based services or the telephone. But the awareness of students cannot be automated, and they may require even more enhanced supports for becoming aware of the staff and courses available. Many institutions personalize this process by providing registration information services that help students to make more informed selections by interacting with tutors, staff and other students about the selections available to them. One undergraduate course in the human services offers students ongoing awareness building meetings in which students discuss their educational experiences in certain substantive areas of the curriculum including research, fieldwork, human development, and individual and group services. These students have opportunities to learn about staff teaching styles, course content and course requirements. They are encouraged to contact members of staff, and the availability of teaching syllabuses online enables them to examine what they can get from a particular staff member.

Certainly these kinds of embellishments to registration put students into new roles as consumers and as customers. Indeed, some staff may feel that they are not only teaching students, but also attracting customers whom they must increasingly satisfy. The publication of staff performance data reinforces these new student roles as consumers and customers. Students in some institutions can access publications that summarize student evaluations of the teaching of members of staff, as well as their scholarly performance. Students can examine how their peers rated these members of staff, and use the ratings as part of their decision making about particular courses.

Awareness building in student life

Awareness building also emerges in student life, particularly in the area of housing. Residential campuses (as opposed to commuter campuses) extend the educational programme from the classroom into the residential living environment. Supports for academic success may involve peer counselling, group work and individualized tutoring. Advanced undergraduate or post-graduate students may staff student housing, helping students to identify their needs, link with academic supports and take advantage of recreational opportunities. Such staff members may become essential intermediaries in interpreting educational policies and practices, and helping students to become aware of the norms they must follow and the expectations they must fulfil. These staff members may foster student support by bringing small groups of students together to learn about the campus and how the educational institution works.

Awareness building becomes the bridge connecting students to the institution of higher or post-secondary education. Institutions must make basic cultural decisions about how formal or informal and impersonal or personal they want awareness building to be for their students. Our experience suggests that the more information these awareness building processes help students to gain, the better. However, our experience also suggests that students need personal interpreters to help them to use this information. These interpreters help students understand their roles and the resources that are available to support their successful execution of these roles.

IMPROVING STUDENT ACCESS

Many institutions focus their efforts on students who are portrayed as 'challenged'. Deaf students, students with different learning styles and needs, and students with physical or emotional challenges are often major groups of focus of accessibility efforts. Another traditional focus is helping students with financial needs to achieve entry to academic courses.

These efforts taken collectively reduce barriers to participation in education, and facilitate the uptake of academic courses, services and facilities. There is a broad array of these access efforts, from priority registration to the availability of note takers, readers and research assistance. Access resources become important when institutions are seeking to increase diversity and be responsive to the needs of students of different cultural, ethnic and socio-economic backgrounds. Many students may fall by the wayside when academic institutions are not responsive to them and the issues their backgrounds create.

Although some students will have needs that require accommodated responses by staff or institution, there do not have to be lower expectations for these students. For example, a staff member with a deaf student in her classroom approached an academic advisor for guidance on how to handle a situation occurring in the classroom. The instructor reported that she asked her class to sit in a circle to encourage communication. The interpreter for the deaf student sat in the middle facing the student. The instructor found this somewhat distracting to the class but chose not to say anything initially until it became obvious that in addition to interpreting, the interpreter and the student were having conversations during the lecture and ensuing class discussion. Not knowing what to do, the instructor asked the advisor about ways to approach this situation. The instructor seemed shocked when the advisor suggested that she handle it as she would for any other student. The interpreter, in this situation, needed to help the student to participate in class to make the lecture and the class discussion accessible.

Teaching staff are critical to making learning experiences accessible to all students who wish to participate as part of their course of study. Accommodations are important aspects of accessibility. Accommodations require some kind of modification to the physical, interpersonal or cultural environment of the learning situation to facilitate the productive participation in an educational experience of those whose characteristics or qualities may exclude them from such participation. Accommodations can come in many different forms and include supportive technology, augmented or modified means of communication, alterations of the physical environment and alterations to how students can demonstrate their learning.

One university encourages staff to offer diverse means by which students can demonstrate their acquisition of essential knowledge and skills. These means include:

- traditional testing and examinations;
- creative and expository writing alternatives;
- visual or schematic portrayals of ideas, concepts and processes, or physical models of ideas, concepts and processes;
- skill-based demonstrations to other students such as workshops or training sessions;
- hands-on portrayals including demonstrations and modelling;
- dramatic performances and accounts;
- oral examination.

The policy of allowing diverse means of demonstrating knowledge acquisition required the staff to explore their own biases about academic performance and to review teaching research on student learning styles. The policy was facilitated by the university's commitment to accessibility and the recognition that increasingly students with different learning backgrounds and qualities were applying and enrolling.

It is not unusual for institutions of higher or post-secondary education to offer an array of services that support the choices students make about their religious affiliations, ethnic and cultural identities, and sexual orientations. As we pointed out in previous chapters, a principal support educational institutions can offer their students is to help them link their social and cultural identities with their emerging identities as students who seek to make contributions to their communities as educated people and professionals.

Other options supporting access include childcare, financial aid, flexible housing arrangements and flexibility in course offerings including location, time of day, number of sections, and self-directed, Internet and distance learning options. Educational institutions with large numbers of students living on their campuses must increasingly respond to the needs of commuting students. Institutions must also increasingly accommodate part-time students, students who work full time and students who have family responsibilities. It is likely that institutional support of access will be a product of the institution's sensitivity, awareness and legitimization of the diversity of its students.

The teaching staff member is a key actor in facilitating the access of students who bring diversity to the educational life of an institution. The staff member links directly to students in a variety of roles, as teacher, mentor, advisor, troubleshooter and principal supporter of students. Staff members can link students to jobs, financial aid resources including scholarships or fellowships, and learning opportunities. They can facilitate classroom-based accommodations, and they can help to find alternative learning resources and ways for students who do not fit into traditional educational structures to demonstrate the acquisition of learning. Accessibility brings us back to the essence of student retention and persistence, which is a product of students forming strong relationships with educators and educational staff, particularly with members of the teaching staff who are devoted to holding on to their students, facilitating their success and helping students to achieve those educational aspirations and outcomes that they find important and valuable.

DEVELOPING AND SUPPORTING STUDENT PERFORMANCE

There is a range of resources, opportunities and programmes that cluster into this area of retention, including remedial educational opportunities and developmental educational services offered to those students whose preparation for higher or post-secondary education may not be strong. However, it is more likely that students possess 'niche' developmental needs, as when a particular student is weak in a specific area and will benefit from help in, for example, oral communication, writing, research, library use, numeracy and mathematics, or computer use. Some institutions may build into the early period of students' education opportunities to redevelop skills that have atrophied during a long absence from education, or even to acquire academic proficiencies other students achieve in secondary school.

Some of these performance-based retention efforts are anticipatory in character. They do not focus on the 'problematic student' whose academic skills may not be strong after admission, but identify promising students in secondary school and begin to work with them in the latter part of secondary school or during the summer before formal enrolment into a technical or undergraduate curriculum. This kind of retention effort facilitates both access and performance, and offers students opportunities to augment targeted skills and competencies before formal entry and have in place an individual plan of academic development that helps them continue to strengthen skills during the early period of post-secondary or higher education.

In several exemplary approaches to retention, institutions of higher or post-secondary education make use of these individualized plans to support students who educators feel are at risk of drop-out. In one model, each student is screened closely based on thorough analyses of the records of their entire secondary and post-secondary careers, with careful assessments revealing critical academic needs that the students and educators must address to support success in education. Special advisors may then help each student to prepare an individualized plan of development and to execute this plan with enriched guidance and access to resources. These advisors assertively monitor and track students, reaching out to them as needed to help them overcome barriers, impasses or problems that can disrupt the achievement of important academic outcomes early in their careers.

In another model, the performance of students is addressed through a peer counselling and group support approach. One advisor is linked to a small group of students who are deemed to be at risk. The programme helps each student to create an individualized plan of development, but this plan is implemented in a group environment in which students meet periodically with their peers to discuss issues, formulate performance strategies, discuss and identify useful resources, and generally support one another. This group support model may be supplemented by volunteer peers, students who have mastered the student role and serve as tutors, advisors and counsellors to group members.

As noted in previous chapters, these kinds of retention supports illustrate that keeping students in higher education is intensively interpersonal and relationship-based. Students do need to be monitored and tracked but not for the purposes of easing them out of the educational institution. Rather, retention efforts that focus on performance need to identify students who struggle academically, assess their situations and develop individualized plans that advance their skills, competencies and proficiencies. The strong relationship between student and advisor, student and group of peers or student and peer advocate are all examples of how relationships can support the monitoring and tracking of students. Successful retention programmes achieve this kind of monitoring and tracking, and offer interventions when the performance of students is problematic.

Some institutions of post-secondary or higher education are wise enough to recognize that students experience performance challenges not only during the early part of their academic careers. These needs can emerge at a number of different points in students' careers. Here are several examples:

- Doctoral students must complete an advanced statistical course in factor analysis. The members of staff teaching these courses are concerned that a number of students lack the basic understanding of linear algebra they need to master the content of the course fully. The staff members offer a short, concentrated module on linear algebra before the beginning of term to prepare students for the statistical content they need to master.
- Students starting a post-graduate course in social sciences receive an intensive course on using a university's library system, requiring demonstration of the mastery of 10 competencies in archival research.
- Students moving from the core curriculum of a liberal arts college to their major areas of study must show that they can apply their core research and writing skills to the preparation of a paper in their academic discipline.

These examples reflect the efforts of an institution and its staff to avoid placing artificial barriers in front of their students. Staff members recognize that higher education is increasingly complex and advanced education builds on competencies students develop during lower-tier courses, in the core curriculum and in their undergraduate studies. Even the brightest students may lack certain competencies, and a good retention infrastructure helps to identify these students and assist them to get the competencies or proficiencies they need to advance in their education and their disciplines.

There is another aspect of performance that is quite intriguing when thinking about student retention and persistence. A number of institutions of post-secondary or higher education are incorporating grievance procedures that enable students to put forth their cases regarding dismissal, the loss of credit or other penalties. Although these procedures recognize that the situation between students and institutions has reached an adversarial juncture, they can be invaluable in revealing student conduct issues that relate to performance or that even originate in performance needs that have gone unassessed and unaddressed. Our experience with student grievances suggests that students often feel they are punished for misunderstanding academic conduct, or for not having a particular skill they felt the academic course should have equipped them with.

For example, in one situation, a student's work had contained plagiarism, something that all students understood would lead to dismissal. The student's grievance indicated that she did not understand why she was dismissed, and that she did not have an understanding of the appropriate and proper manner of using the material of published scholars. An interview with the student showed that she did not understand these conventions and their ethical implications. She produced other examples of her work that contained plagiarism but that had not resulted in her dismissal, and she was able to show that previous staff members had overlooked these improprieties.

This situation resulted in an audit of the institution's teaching content and its approach to teaching ethical conduct in research. The audit revealed that members were not giving this educational content due consideration in their courses, and a small module on the ethical use of research and published materials was introduced into three core courses.

Grievances are extreme situations, often fraught with conflict, anger and finger pointing. But they can reveal retention needs, and it is important for institutions to pay attention to what each grievance says about the performance of a student, and to consider how the problems that bring a student to a grievance could be addressed earlier in the educational career.

FACILITATING THE TRANSITION OF STUDENTS

Coming into an institution of higher education, moving through one, and moving out of one into work or additional education and training all involve the transition of students from one setting to another, from one role or status to another and from one kind of performance situation to another. These transitions are an important aspect of student retention and persistence, and the retention efforts of educational institutions are consciously identifying and responding to these transitions and addressing the problems they can create for students. Transitions are an important focal point for retention because they create new expectations, performance demands and resource requirements that some students cannot address or resolve successfully on their own. Take, for example, these four transitions:

- A student wants to complete her undergraduate education by entering an upper-tier university after the completion of the first two years at a local college. She has serious financial constraints and is contemplating postponing her education for three years until she can work and earn the money she needs to continue.
- A student wants to do a post-graduate course in psychology. She arrives at this decision late in her undergraduate career. Her undergraduate subject is literature, which does not equip her with the core courses she needs for entrance into a doctoral course of study.
- An undergraduate student finds that he will soon be a father. He is unprepared for this role, and he is anxious about splitting his time between parenting, two part-time jobs and full-time enrolment in a professional engineering course.
- An undergraduate student of Arab-American heritage finds himself moving from a closely knit ethnic and cultural enclave to a very large, diverse university campus. He finds himself isolated and lonely.

All of these are transitions, and they are all of a different kind. One transition is financial in nature, another one is career-oriented and another involves family life and parenting. Still another involves culture and the accommodation to a new kind of environment in which a young man's cultural group is only one of the many groups represented in the institution. Sensitivity to these transitions requires each institution of higher or post-secondary education to understand its students and to understand what kinds of life transitions they are negotiating.

Why is sensitivity to these transitions so important? The social science literature is full of research demonstrating that transitions in life, and in settings and situations, can create new kinds of expectations or demands. In turn these expectations and demands can create considerable stress. Students handle stress in different ways. Some students internalize it, and do not share what is happening to them and the toll it is taking personally, interpersonally and ultimately academically. Some students externalize it. They may become problematic or difficult, creating conflict for their peers, staff and administrative personnel. Other students may navigate transitions quite well, moving into new settings, situations and roles without any problem.

As with other supports for student retention and persistence that facilitate awareness, accessibility and performance, the facilitation of transition is most successful when students have available to them strong advice and counselling relationships. Advisors help students to identify their needs and the challenges they face, and to assist them to master these challenges and to move on in their academic careers successfully. Some students will need more of this support from advisors than will others. Nonetheless, a good advice and counselling service, as we underscore in Chapter 6, is probably the most powerful tool an institution can offer its students to achieve student retention and persistence. The advisor is the cornerstone of student development, student mastery of the academic role and the troubleshooting of challenges, issues and needs, and a critical building block of the infrastructure of retention and persistence.

Support for successful transition is undertaken by institutions of post-secondary and higher education somewhat differently depending on how broadly they conceive their mission of retention, and the scope of the support systems they offer to their students. For example, Web pages may present resources and opportunities for students to integrate family life and education. An institution's sensitivity to parental and family responsibilities and the role change inherent in becoming a parent may result in substantive supports. For example, an urban university may offer parenting courses to its students, and linkages to health care resources that offer prenatal, neonatal, paediatric and adolescent medical services.

There are other strategies institutions of post-secondary or higher education employ to facilitate the transition of their students. These include:

- enhanced support of students who are living on their own for the first time;
- assistance in the transition from lower to higher courses;

- assistance in decision making about the selection of an area of study, concentration or specialization;
- opportunities to convert required undergraduate courses after enrolment into post-graduate or professional courses;
- outreach to students of particular ethnic, religious or cultural backgrounds;
- assistance to transition into various work opportunities, trial work opportunities or co-operative education;
- assistance to transition from one subject to another;
- assistance to transition from school to career.

Relating persistence and retention to the current interest among students in career development and career mobility can offer another focus for the transition efforts of institutions of higher and post-secondary education. The involvement of students in career and career transition can begin immediately upon their entry into a post-secondary course. The idea of career can help students to make sense of the choices, decisions and transitions they face. The construct of career development unfolds in several stages and the execution of each stage by students takes them further in strengthening their vocational choices, their identities as educated professionals and their roles as educated citizens.

The Web pages of several institutions of higher or post-secondary education highlight career outcomes at each step of the educational process. For example, one institution links lower-level courses to career exploration, and students are helped to achieve a career direction by the end of their core curriculum educational experience. Academic content is integrated with career content. Students are both challenged and supported in their exploration of career paths, their trial work and vocational experiences, and their tentative decisions about an academic and career direction. Some institutions link classroom and career through community service that offers students first-hand exposure to learning about themselves through service, which also earns them academic credit. Some institutions offer ongoing co-operative work experiences while others organize their curricula according to both academic content and career-relevant project content.

These efforts, no matter how diverse, share a common aim: to help students connect their evolution of self with their academic and career preparation. Career exploration at the beginning of post-secondary education can link to the other career development stages involving choice and commitment. Career choice and commitment are dynamic, and they emerge at different times in the lives of students. Nonetheless, they are important transitions leading students to one of the most significant outcomes of their education, a commitment to an initial vocation. This initial commitment may further evolve within one career path, but will more probably initiate students into the world of professional work, and form a springboard into other career pathways that may return them to some form of higher or post-secondary education in the future. As already emphasized the 'one education, one career' imperative is a concept of the past. Students are preparing for a future of unanticipated opportunities, new work opportunities and new career pathways. Student retention and persistence are relevant in the light of equipping students with a broader conception of their education than simply getting a degree or adequately meeting academic requirements.

CONCLUSION: A FRAMEWORK OF THE INFRASTRUCTURE OF STUDENT RETENTION AND PERSISTENCE

The content of this chapter suggests a framework of the infrastructure of supporting student retention and persistence within any institution of higher or post-secondary education. Figure 5.1 presents this framework. It brings together two dimensions: the four *principal functions of retention*, which are awareness, accessibility, performance and transition; and three *forms of critical interactions* that support retention, which are formal programmes, staff–student interactions and student–student interactions.

	Formal Programmes	Staff–Student Interactions	Student–Student Interactions
Awareness			
Accessibility			
Performance			
Transition			

Figure 5.1 *A framework of the infrastructure of student retention and persistence*

The *awareness building function* assists students to learn about how higher or post-secondary education operates, and how they can get involved as success-ful students. Students do this by interacting with formal programmes that help orient them to the expectations, resources and opportunities of higher education, with staff who help them as tutors to understand how to achieve success in classes, projects and other educational opportunities, with other students who offer mutual support and peer advice or counselling options, and with community gatekeepers who help them to become aware of education and its importance to their personal, financial and social success.

The *access function* helps students who experience intractable barriers to over-come them and to achieve success academically. Specific programmes facilitate access, while the advocacy and counselling of staff assist students to obtain the resources they need to perform the role of student adequately. Interactions with other students may facilitate a strong sense of identity and strengthen resolve to remain in education, and interactions with community agencies can result in tangible resources like a job or financial assistance to make higher or post-secondary education possible.

Helping students to achieve academically lies within the domain of the *performance function*. Students interact with programmes that help them to address and achieve substantive academic competencies (eg developmental education), and they interact with staff through advice, tutorials and mentoring to get the assistance they need to master required content. This function can also come into play as students interact with their peers through couns-elling, tutorials and role modelling mediated through individual and group support sessions. And this function expresses itself when community volunteers, social service personnel and members of ethnic, religious and other organizations offer mentoring to students who may be struggling with perfor-mance issues.

The *transition function* can be implemented through the organization of formal programmes that support successful transitions on the part of students, such as when students are helped to learn about career options, and obtain opportunities to observe, experience and try out these options. The transition function can be seen when staff members help students to learn about post-grad-uate options, and how to put together a good application to their next educa-tional choice. Students organizing interest groups that focus on substantive career and academic areas can facilitate the transition of students to new work, educa-tional or career roles. And community groups that offer students opportunities to investigate and experience new educational opportunities, such as scholarships or fellowships supporting travel, research and self-directed learning, can facilitate transition.

This framework does underscore a theme that we intentionally develop in this book. Retention is not reactive. Keeping students in higher or post-secondary education is developmental and supportive and, as a result, it is proactive. It builds on interactions and relationships that are geared to the needs of each student, and that assist each student to make the commitments and choices that result in success. It is these interactions and relationships that form the essence of retention. We cannot separate retention from student development. And, so, it is to the process of student development that we now turn our attention.

6

Student development and its implications for retention

MAIN POINTS OF THE CHAPTER

- Proactive approaches to retention facilitate student development by: 1) anticipating the needs of students early in their higher or post-secondary educational careers; 2) tracking and monitoring students on an ongoing basis; 3) assisting students to identify their educational aspirations and offering them opportunities to explore these and test them out; and 4) offering comprehensive resources that decrease stress and facilitate performance.
- Proactive approaches link retention and persistence to student development and this requires individualization for each student.
- There is extensive variation across students in terms of their development, which in turn requires different responses to foster academic success.
- The basis of student development lies in a student's mastery of the role of the student. Thus, students need insight into and an understanding of what is expected of them and how to behave in a manner that produces successful educational outcomes.
- The role of student varies by type of educational course and by educational setting. Thus, students enrolled in lower-level technical colleges may have very different roles compared to doctoral students in post-graduate research institutions. But the role of student is defined by educational norms, standards, expectations, requirements, duties and, ultimately, outcomes.

- A retention effort that develops students in a proactive manner helps students to become aware of the student role; understand what is expected and required of them; take action to master the role; and transform into successful students.
- Advisors and the advice and counselling system are fundamental to student development. Advisors help students develop their life plans and incorporate into these plans their educational outcomes. They also assist students to test these plans and to evaluate them based on their aspirations and aims.

When thinking of retention it is too easy to fall into a reactive frame of reference in which the retention effort is mobilized or otherwise comes into play when the student demonstrates or experiences problems, usually of an academic nature. Reactive approaches to retention delay intervention, and may be slow to respond to the needs of students because they fail to anticipate the issues or concerns many students present in post-secondary or higher education. Reactive retention programmes can be very segmented and limited, only coming into play in matters pertaining to academic performance or academic adjustment. It is as if these approaches to retention assume that all students have the competencies and capabilities to perform effectively in institutions of post-secondary or higher education and, therefore, retention efforts must be reserved for only those who prove to be most problematic.

We do not want to condemn this kind of approach out of hand. However, we do want to emphasize that those reactive retention approaches and the programmes they foster are not the foundation of effective programmes, as many of the vignettes we presented in previous chapters highlight.

Alternatively, proactive approaches to retention emphasize early intervention into student situations and do not postpone working with students until they experience very serious situations that compromise their status and continued enrolment. Proactive approaches to retention tend to take a comprehensive and developmental approach to the student. They assume that many students need and can benefit from an organized and intentional effort to help them to be successful in post-secondary and higher education. These approaches are not limited to the academic sphere alone but extend beyond this to address the many barriers students can experience that can disrupt their enrolment and involvement in higher education, and their success as students.

At the heart of proactive approaches to retention lies a commitment to the development of students so that they will and can be successful in the educational course and setting of their choosing. This chapter links retention to student development, and asserts that the most proactive approach to retention lies in individualizing the development of each and every student. This individualization recognizes that the student's previous educational, social and cultural, and personal background offers strengths and assets on which to base retention, as well as suggests specific needs that must be met in order to increase the likelihood that persistence and retention occur.

No student comes completely 'developed' to engage in post-secondary and higher education, but some students are more than ready to take advantage of higher education and to find their place as successful students in the educational milieu. Others, however, are not well developed in these regards and they require considerable attention inside and outside the institution if they are going to be successful. Thus, there is variation across students, and it is up to the retention effort and programme to broaden its boundaries to match useful approaches to student development that meet the scope of the needs of various students. As previously stated, proactive retention is about making good matches between what students need and the supports the institution of post-secondary or higher education offers to facilitate their success.

THE BASIS OF STUDENT DEVELOPMENT

We employ the idea of development as a principal quality of retention because of the important involvement members of the academic community share in helping students reach their potential and to find their niche as citizens who contribute socially, culturally, economically and interpersonally to the quality of life of a community and a society. This is quite a job but not an unreasonable one. Many post-secondary academic institutions pride themselves in this mission and often highlight the critical role they play in helping to enrich and develop each student. Student development is part of the institutional framework of these academic settings, and part of the core responsibilities of staff, administrators and student service personnel in those progressive institutions that frame the development of students as a principal aim of academic service.

As Figure 6.1 illustrates, the facilitation of student development focuses on fostering academic maturity. Students develop an increased capacity to manage their own learning experience as they move from academic foundations to purposeful learning and then to autonomous learning. As the students evolve their persistence increases and retention risks decrease.

Student development to some may seem like a very demanding if not impossible task. A member of staff in physical science may wonder whether she should or can be involved in such an undertaking. A member of teaching staff once said to one of the authors: 'This kind of student involvement is best left up to counsellors. It's their job to worry about whether each student gets what they need. It's my job to teach and to research.' We cannot overemphasize how important it is for *all* members of the academic community to think proactively about their contributions to student development, even when this means that staff members

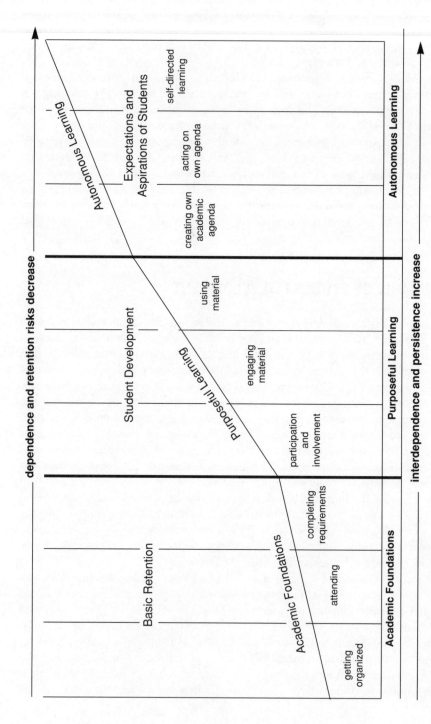

Figure 6.1 *Academic maturity*

must reframe or otherwise think differently about their role. Keeping students in higher education cannot be left to a few members of staff or to specialized staff. It takes a community of higher education to hold on to students.

Here is an example. As an undergraduate student, one of the authors worked for a year as a groundskeeping assistant on the university campus. The head of groundskeeping offered employment to many students who needed student financial aid. He was receptive to helping students with problems, and developed relationships across campus and outside of campus to help students resolve them. Indeed, he was very proactive, and met individually with students to discuss how they were to balance their obligations as students and as workers. He was adamant that his 'student workers' would be successful as students, and his resolve paid off. Many of them achieved success and he was instrumental in this outcome.

This story illustrates the idea identified in Chapter 3. The institutional mission of retention does need to recognize that retention roles are pervasive and cut across many areas of institutional life. The groundskeeper's commitment to the success of his students could strike us as puzzling. What was the basis of his commitment? He would joke with his student workers and say, 'What good are clean grounds if there are no students to make a mess of them?' This was a man who had committed 20 years of his working life to maintaining, grooming and nurturing the grounds of the university. He saw himself as a member of the academic community, and he understood the mission of the university in a tacit manner. From his perspective, the university was there to serve students.

This story also brings to light the basis of student development. There are risks in oversimplifying this important concept, yet nonetheless it serves as a useful way of thinking about an idea that can be quite complex. *The basis of student development lies in a student's mastery of the role of student.* Institutions of post-secondary and higher education often include the full development and enrichment of students as part of their mission, but they cannot even begin to achieve this until they engage in the most fundamental aspect of student development, which is the facilitation of the student's mastery of the role of student. The groundskeeper understood this. He knew that he was not supervising or training permanent groundskeepers. He was making higher education accessible to students through part-time employment. He understood that their mastery of their roles as students was paramount to the success of the academic institution. To do this, he helped them to balance work and academic life.

THE ROLE OF STUDENT

What is the student role? There are many aspects, but it can be broken down in a manner that helps illuminate its constituent elements. The 'role of student' involves norms, standards, performance expectations, requirements and duties that the institution frames, prioritizes and applies. These adhere to the status of the student, that is, to the position of the student in the institution of post-secondary or higher education. This status and the related role constellation will vary by *type of educational course* and by *educational setting*. Undergraduate students, for example, have different statuses and roles compared to post-graduate students. Even within undergraduate education there may be differences between those in the early stages and those in the later stages of their higher education. There may also be differences within post-graduate education.

The setting may be critical to defining and conceiving of student status and role. For example, students at small colleges or universities may have a range of independent study options, projects and individualized study from which to select. These options may place them in intensive interaction with teaching staff, requiring students and teachers to reframe the nature and substance of their relationship. Upper-level students at large universities may have smaller seminars and classes than students in lower-level courses, but the sheer size of the institution may preclude more individualized and intensive educational alternatives. Local colleges may offer different statuses and accompanying roles than traditional colleges and universities.

Differences in the setting of higher or post-secondary education can foster differences in status and role, and these can be important to understanding the norms, standards, performance expectations, requirements and duties an institution assigns to the student role. Indeed, the student role as a factor in retention may be so important that it influences the success of students in making productive or effective transitions from one setting to another.

The effect of transitions on student role

There are numerous transitions students make from one institutional setting to another (eg from local college to university), from one status to another (eg from school student to college student, or from undergraduate student to post-graduate student), from one course to another (eg from general syllabus to single subject), from one type of education to another (eg classroom lectures to individualized projects), or from one stage of a course to another (eg from doctoral course work to dissertation).

Each of these transitions represents a change in student role involving perhaps new norms, standards, performance expectations, requirements and duties. A transition means that students need to learn new content regarding these roles, new levels of performance, and even new attitudes, knowledge and skills. From our experience, role transitions create persistence and retention challenges, and can result in a heightened sense of stress on the part of students that requires the creation of new supports or the extension of current supports.

Some examples of role transition are useful here:

- Jose was successful in his first two years at a local college, and transferred to a university to complete his undergraduate education. The expectations of staff at the university were very different from those of staff at the college. Jose found that teaching staff expected him to work independently, and when he sought help the staff member assigned him to a peer tutor. He had to learn to work on his own or with a tutor rather than directly with a member of staff as he had previously.

- As an outstanding undergraduate student, Sally proved that she had the academic preparation to be successful in law school. The close, supportive culture of her undergraduate college was conducive to her learning style. She enjoyed small classes, independent studies and learning experiences through the research of her tutor. Sally chose a prestigious law school at a major university. She says that this law school was 'an eye-opener'. She was not prepared for the large lecture courses, the remoteness of the teaching staff, the Socratic teaching method and the competitiveness of her fellow students. At the end of her first term, Sally's grades were poor.

- Sam thought he was a good writer. He demonstrated to his instructors in his introductory language and creative writing courses that he aspired to a career as a writing teacher or author. His passion was composition, and his performance in the core writing courses was outstanding. He decided to transfer to another college known for its advanced composition courses, aiming to refine his craft. But he soon found out that his fellow students were stronger than him, and that the teaching staff's expectations of his work and their standards far exceeded Sam's appraisal of himself as a writer. He became quite demoralized and thought about leaving his new college after investing a great deal of money and time to make this transition.

- Ashaka is in the last stage of her doctoral course, the dissertation. She is very much on her own since her course does not facilitate dissertation research by linking advanced doctoral students to staff mentors who have a strong research agenda in areas of student interest. She completed her qualifying exams and is now having a very difficult time carrying out her dissertation research. She gets very little support and assistance from teaching staff, and she feels it is time now to quit her studies and start work before she actually begins her dissertation research.

All four of these individuals were good students, and all showed potential for success in higher education. Indeed, all four demonstrated effectiveness in student roles before they made transitions to either new institutions and/or to new phases of their education. Jose transferred from a local college to a university known for its research focus. He was not prepared for the new culture, and the university was not effective in helping students who had transferred to learn how this culture worked. Jose's status as a university student is in jeopardy, even though he has a strong academic record.

Sally was in a similar situation. She found that her chosen law school lacked the attributes that helped her to thrive in her undergraduate education. Unfortunately, even though she was a promising student, she chose to leave law school because its culture was not supportive of the way she wanted to learn.

Sam found himself in a new pool of students all of whom had been attracted from far and wide to the university's advanced creative writing course because of its outstanding reputation. He could no longer evaluate his writing in relationship to other students taking introductory courses, many of whom did not plan careers in creative writing. He was in a new peer and reference group requiring him to aspire to higher expectations or standards. The course did not help prepare him for this challenge and left it up to him to work out how to realign his expectations, given his new status and role as an aspiring creative writer.

Ashaka found herself in a new phase of her course that required autonomy and independence. She did not know whether she was prepared to handle her dissertation. Neither the teaching staff nor anyone else in the institution helped her to navigate this critical transition in the career of a doctoral student.

We can see in each of these vignettes how setting interacts with student roles to influence students' conceptions of themselves. Transition is important in these examples since it is the transitions that amplify standards, performance expectations, requirements and duties. For example, in Jose's situation he discovered that the school he chose held high expectations for student independence, autonomy and self-help. He could not rely on the conception of staff–student relationships that he had learnt previously. Sam found that he needed to perform in a new way, not as an undergraduate student, but as an aspiring creative writer.

Institutional support

All four of these students found themselves in situations in which they had to master new roles. Some institutions require students to make the changes necessary to be successful. However, those institutions that possess a strong orientation to retention will expand their conception of role change. They understand how important it is to facilitate a student's mastery of the student role and to make explicit as much as possible the standards, performance expectations, requirements and duties that go with the role of student. It becomes apparent that the depth and diversity of the supports available through the institution to help students to master these roles successfully are integrated into the retention effort as principal features.

The five supports outlined in Chapter 1 (emotional support and sustenance, informational support, instrumental support, material support and identity support) become important tools when the institution of post-secondary or higher education positions them to facilitate the mastery of the student role. Each support offers something to the student in relationship to the mastery of the student role:

- Emotional support helps students to address the anxiety or fears the student role creates, and helps students to address the uncertainties that role changes or transitions can induce.
- Informational support offers students concrete information about what the institution requires of them as students and how they need to perform.
- Instrumental support helps students to resolve specific problems or issues that can emerge in the institution, within their specific educational courses and outside the institution, through hands-on help and advice or even technical assistance.
- Material support offers students the concrete resources they need in order to master roles. Here financial help, transportation and assistance in securing books and equipment may be important to successful mastery.
- Identity support can facilitate a transformation in the student's sense of self to incorporate values, perspectives and conceptions of self that are consistent with the aims of the educational course.

So, Ashaka gets the support she needs to navigate the transition to the dissertation successfully as well as support to help her to complete it in a timely manner. Here we can see the importance of identity support to Ashaka's situation. Her new identity as a dissertation student is quite different from the identity she possessed when completing her doctoral course work. The programme may put in place a face-to-face or virtual support system that helps her to make this transition through group support from selected staff and other dissertation students.

Student development is based on mastery of the student role. It is developmental because the institution, through its approach to persistence and retention, helps students to acquire the attitudes, knowledge or know-how, skills and motivation to meet the demands the student role creates for them. An educational institution may offer this kind of socialization at milestone points in the career of students. These milestones may come when students are contemplating a change in role at the points of entry, the selection of a course or subject, career selection, re-decision about a subject or course, planning for the further advancement of their education or progressing to the world of work. Helping students to master the role of student may constitute either a formal or an informal curriculum that the educational institution designs to help students to gain insight into how the college works, or how the culture of the institution operates.

Helping students to master this role can lead to some very important developmental outcomes. Marge, for example, does not have a strong academic self-concept. She was a homemaker for almost 20 years, beginning college at the age of 40 after a divorce. She wants an education to help her to launch a career at mid-life, but has no idea how a university works. Her close friends never attended college, her former husband did not attend and she is the first in her family to pursue higher education. She likes business, and believes that a career in accounting will help her use what she feels to be a natural aptitude with numbers.

Marge selects a local university that started as a business and secretarial college but expanded to offer business curricula at undergraduate and post-graduate levels. The university is very sensitive to the needs of older students and has designed a full term of academic work that prepares students to learn how to be business students. The course focuses on helping students to improve their confidence, and to begin to craft professional self-concepts as business professionals. Four major components of this curriculum frame the activities of the first term. These are:

- *Awareness and contemplation.* The curriculum helps students to gain an awareness of the educational options available to them, and the academic and intellectual competencies each option requires of students. It helps them to contemplate the various options and choices that are available to them in business education.
- *Understanding and commitment.* The curriculum assists each student to gain an understanding of how the curriculum operates and the demands the educational institution places on students in terms of performance expectations, requirements and standards. It helps students to frame their initial commitment fully aware that they can make other choices if they wish.
- *Action in support of mastery.* Students have structured opportunities to begin to master the role of business student by revisiting their academic preparation and strengthening core competencies in computer literacy, numeracy, reading and writing.
- *Transformation.* Students are guided through a process that assists them to transform themselves from applicants to students who are successfully involved in business course work and learning activities. This involves the transformation of staff–student relationships, the business of the classroom and duties pertaining to the conduct of learning as a business enterprise.

Through this course, Marge builds her self-confidence as a student. She forms enduring relationships with other students and establishes a working relationship with at least two members of staff who are available to her as mentors. By the end of the first term, she has consulted these members of staff through face-to-face meetings, e-mail and Web page communications. Although she feels that she has a long way to go in building her confidence, she says that she has a good grasp of how to succeed as an undergraduate business student at the institution of her choice.

There is one other consideration that is important to student development through mastery of the student role, and Marge's preparatory work reflects it. It involves the *congruence* between the requirements and expectations of the student role and students' conceptions of themselves. We have found that an institution that commits itself to facilitating a student's mastery of the student role will also facilitate better decision making on the part of students regarding whether they want to persist or find an alternative opportunity for themselves through perhaps employment or a different kind of educational option.

Students need opportunities to appraise the correspondence or discrepancy between role requirements and their own values, perspectives and needs. Thus, not only helping students to learn about the student role and what it requires but also supporting them in making active appraisals about themselves and this role can result in students making stronger commitments or alternative decisions about their involvement, aims and destinies in post-secondary or higher education.

THE ROLE OF THE ADVISOR IN STUDENT DEVELOPMENT

What advisors and the advice and counselling system can do on behalf of students

Some of the most important relationships for students are with advisors. Whether the issue is academic, career, personal, financial, medical or social, advisors can prove invaluable in providing resources or direction to ensure a positive outcome. Indeed, it may be the advisor who is instrumental in the personalization of the student's experience in higher education. By 'advisor', we do not mean the person who only advises students about their academic courses. Advisors can include members of the teaching staff, administrators, student development personnel, student service personnel and leaders of non-academic student activities. They may be situated inside or outside the institutions. They are individuals who dedicate themselves to helping students. They work with students to make critical choices and decisions about higher education, to find and take advantage of opportunities that help students develop in their chosen fields and academic pursuits, and to troubleshoot those issues that can disrupt students' involvement and success in higher education.

Advisors are not always aware of the influence they have on the students with whom they work, and at times the feedback they receive from their advisees about what makes their services effective may surprise them. Some students may tell their advisors that it was important to know that someone was available to help them if they needed it. Others may remember the important interventions an advisor undertook to help them resolve academic, income, employment or housing difficulties. Although students may enter college with specific aims, they may not always know how to achieve these aims. Some students simply do not know how to utilize resources, especially in large universities. It is here that advisors may serve their most important function, that is, in helping students to get an understanding of how to navigate the institution, take advantage of opportunities, sustain themselves during periods of stress, cope with being students and perform successfully as students.

A student in a large university once remarked about her experience as a new student coming from a small secondary school:

> I walked into a large lecture hall for my chemistry class and was confronted by over 100 people. I was shocked since there were only 15 people in my school chemistry class. Even worse, after the lecture ended, I left the hall using the back exit instead of the way I had entered, and was completely lost. I had no idea where I was. It took me so long to get used to the structure of the university not to mention finding the libraries, my classes, the financial aid office and even knowing how to get an advisor let alone how to find out who my advisor was at that time.

Unfortunately, the university did not help this student to make one of the most important connections early in her academic experience, that is, linking up with someone who could help her acclimatize to the university.

This student's experience is not uncommon. Having a connection with someone within the university can make the difference between having a good and bad experience in college, or between staying and leaving. The advisor is one important and concrete connection between the student and the university, and can help personalize the educational institution. Quickly linking students with a person who can provide support and guidance can lead to greater success and can keep students from withdrawing when things get difficult. Fostering these links may be one of the most important retention tactics an institution of post-secondary or higher education can take in the support of its students. One of the first important student development outcomes of advice and counselling services is helping students to stay enrolled and to persist in their education. Without this foundation subsequent student development becomes impossible.

Proactive support

Proactive advice services are difficult to achieve when many advisees will only seek out their advisors when they are in trouble or perhaps when they are in a crisis. Thus, advisors serve an important function in framing how students use the service and in defining when they should use it. Helping students to understand its proactive use is an important function. The system can incorporate specific tactics to facilitate its proactive use as a student support system. A proactive system:

- undertakes an institution-wide information campaign to alert students to the availability of advisors and how to trigger involvement with advisors;
- offers students opportunities to designate their own advisor and, therefore, expand the range of individuals, programmes and roles that can serve in advice and counselling.

- reaches out to individual students and identifies the needs of each one of them;
- forms strong and enduring relationships with students that are positive in tone;
- helps students to gain an understanding of the roles they must master and to gain insight into how the educational course 'works';
- assists students to gain insight into student role expectations, requirements and duties;
- assists students to identify the needs and supports they require so they can achieve success as students;
- facilitates students' use of resources that fulfils their needs and helps them to be successful in the student role;
- keeps the door open to students, and legitimizes keeping in touch and friendly visiting;
- makes advice services easy to trigger, informal in nature, and continuously and flexibly available in terms of time, location and method (eg phone, e-mail, Web site).

How advisors facilitate student development

Preparing students to come into college and use its resources can be a major component of student development. Cultural factors, lack of awareness of resources, and previous habits of coping and help seeking can act as barriers that prevent students from asking for and using assistance. Advice service efforts have to consider personalized work with students who are new to the 'college scene'. 'New' here does not only mean early in the higher education career of students. 'New' also refers to those students for whom higher education is novel and mystifying since they do not have role models available to them in their families or social networks to help them gain an understanding of college and how it works.

This kind of advice service goes beyond the traditional supports where students are provided with a plan of work as they decide on an academic subject or course, or prepare for a professional course. Advisors here serve as navigators or guides helping students to 'learn the ropes' of higher education. They assist students to accommodate or acclimatize to the culture of higher education.

Universities wanting to ensure success for their students must look at the diversity of students entering college. Institutions of higher education must consider non-traditional groups and understand their needs. For many of these students, higher education becomes a choice born of necessity: to enter a profession in an attempt to improve their socio-economic status and life circumstances; to achieve a dream; or to respond to family or group pressures. Advice services must take into consideration why students feel that they need higher education. Indeed, one of the most potent development outcomes an advisor can help a student to achieve is to gain insight into how higher education fits into the student's life plan.

In serving as navigators or guides, advisors facilitate students' exploration of opportunities that promote both development and retention. These can include financial aid, career awareness and choice, housing, student health services, child-care and involvement in campus or other student life activities. The advisor should expect to be a major force in the life of some students for it is not unusual for students to lack the support of parents and family both financially and emotionally. They will need support and encouragement as they develop a plan to pursue their particular course of study and as they continue to evaluate this in relationship to what they want to achieve in higher education and how higher education fits into their life plan. Thus, other features of proactive advice services that foster student development emerge here. The advice and counselling system assists students to:

- clarify their life plans;
- review and appraise their life plans as they move through their educational experience;
- match their life plans as they emerge or as they are framed with their educational direction, aspirations and aims.

As students explore various educational opportunities and courses, they will need assistance in the clarification of their educational aspirations, their expectations about their education and whether these expectations can be met through their choice of educational courses. Success in the early stages for students as they pursue their interests will lead to a feeling of belonging. They will feel as though they are part of the institution when the institution respects the questions and issues they present and they find that the institution takes seriously, and seeks to fulfil, their interests, needs and aspirations. It is likely that a feeling of belonging will lead to student commitment. This in turn will result in persistence and ultimately retention.

Helping each student to 'belong' is probably the essence of personalization, and it is the advisor who can give this personal accent to an institution that many students might otherwise find remote or even uncaring. Perhaps the ultimate outcomes of student development lie in assisting all students to belong in the institution and to make a personal commitment to their education.

Outcomes of advice and counselling: an illustrative case

The case of Maysoon illustrates the importance of advice and counselling as a student development process to subsequent success in the role of student. Maysoon came to the advisor to discuss the possibility of applying for a post-graduate course. She was apprehensive because of her low average grades. She wanted to pursue a post-graduate degree against her family's wishes. She had originally wanted to pursue a social science degree as her first degree, but her family was intent on her obtaining a degree in preparation for a career in health sciences. She started a pharmacy degree at her parents' insistence and ended with very poor grades in many of the hard science classes. After three years, she gave up, withdrew from the course and finished a general bachelor degree so that she could graduate.

When she came in to discuss pursuing a post-graduate degree, she prefaced the discussion with an explanation of her cultural background and her family's disapproval of her decision to pursue this degree. She also commented on her previous achievements, indicating that her low grades were not reflective of her potential and she wanted an opportunity to demonstrate her abilities and to be allowed to apply for the post-graduate course.

Maysoon and the advisor discussed the absence of her family's support. She said they would not understand why she had chosen this field and would be concerned that she would not make a lot of money or have status and prestige in their community.

Students like Maysoon face isolation while pursuing a career that is not accepted by their families. Supports within the university become very important to such students as they struggle to pursue their dreams while working to resolve differences within their families. Teaching staff and advisors have to be careful not to judge families when they encounter these kinds of situations. The result could be alienation of the student who might feel that his or her family and culture are misunderstood. Family response in the context of culture and ethnicity needs to be evaluated to develop the best plan to aid the student.

During one of the early advising sessions, Maysoon's mother, brother and maternal aunt came to the advising session to learn about her choice. Though somewhat taken by surprise, the advisor was able to see the strength of the family as they attempted to ensure Maysoon's well-being. In turn the family was able to ask questions and gain a better appreciation of the course.

The advisor and Maysoon clarified her life plan and how post-graduate education in the social sciences fitted into this plan. They reflected on the nature of the social sciences and Maysoon's lifelong interest in them, which was enriched by her interest in the influence of culture on human development. Maysoon investigated the role of post-graduate student in social sciences, and explored career options. She was able to see that a viable career in the social sciences was possible, and that she could earn status within her social group as an educator and researcher.

Maysoon achieved one of the first outcomes of the advice and counselling process. She felt that she belonged in the institution, that she belonged in the social sciences and that her academic choice made personal sense. A second outcome followed a few months later. Maysoon was very committed to her academic and career choice and, when her family sensed this commitment, they relaxed their criticisms and became very supportive of her career direction.

ILLUSTRATIVE VIGNETTES OF LINKING ADVICE AND COUNSELLING TO STUDENT SITUATIONS

Other examples highlight the importance of appreciating student situations and of understanding how to develop students while helping them overcome the barriers they face in their personal situations and helping them to develop the supports they require in order to achieve their own educational aims. Student development must not focus only on where students are going, but also on the barriers that can frustrate their achievement of this destination.

Indeed, student development must be thought of as involving:

1. the identification and clarification of the educational aims of students based on their own aspirations and life plan;
2. an understanding of the personal situations of students;
3. the creation of the emotional, informational, instrumental, material or identity supports identified in Chapter 1 to assist students to test these aims, revise them if they choose and achieve them as much as possible; and
4. troubleshooting and resolution of barriers that can undermine performance of the student role.

Consider these examples:

- John is a 46-year-old who chose to return to college to change careers. He remortgaged his home, saved money for two years and started a post-graduate course. After the first year, he suffered a heart attack and was in hospital. He started to recover and was back on his feet within four months. Proactive advice and counselling enabled him to co-ordinate his recovery with the resumption of his academic career.
- Tony left a career in computers to pursue a degree in human services on a full-time basis. His wife, who strongly supported his decision, chose to work while he was enrolled. In the last term of his degree, Tony's wife was diagnosed with breast cancer, and he was devastated. She began treatment and was given a good prognosis. Tony's advisor assisted him to navigate this family crisis, and to continue his studies without interruption.
- Betty applied for a post-graduate degree upon the completion of her first degree. She had moved away from home and was 'finding' herself for the first time. She began to question her sexual orientation and attended support groups for gay/lesbian/bisexual students on campus. She was unsure of what she wanted, felt depressed and was not putting a lot of time into her course work. Fearing she was jeopardizing her degree, she sought out her advisor to discuss her feelings and options. The advisor assisted her to take a year out, and

worked with the head of her course to facilitate her re-entry and subsequent graduation.

- Jessica took a course that involved an element of practical fieldwork. When she began her practical, she felt she had to prove herself. It was not until she was told that she was at risk of failing the practical that she approached one of her teachers. It was found that she was having a hard time doing her assignments in the practical, and that she had difficulty writing anything without spelling errors or transposing letters and numbers. In a meeting with her advisor, she noted that often the assignments for her course work were proof-read three or four times by various family members, while in the practical, she had to submit her first attempt. The advisor raised the possibility of a learning disability and made arrangements for her to get tested at the university's educational accessibility office. The advisor worked with the practical site to make accommodations that allowed Jessica to perform effectively.

- Peter was on his own for a number of years, having lost contact with his family in his late teens. At the age of 42, he knew that going to college was going to be a long haul. He tried to prepare by saving some money, and he quit his job so that he could focus on his classes. The stress of college quickly resulted in some serious problems for Peter. A member of staff smelt alcohol on his breath, and he lost his apartment. He approached the department head for an emergency loan when he was living out of his car. The advisor helped him to get the financial resources he needed to continue in education, and also assisted him to stabilize his housing situation and seek help for his use of alcohol.

These stories are but a few of the many examples of situations that students face as they struggle to stay in education. When students approach university officials, often the first option is to counsel them out of their courses, giving them the message that they are not able to handle the load, that they are not 'college material' or that they are not ready to handle college because of their life situations. These responses can only push out those students who are excellent candidates for higher education but who require proactive ways of helping them to master their life situations while supporting the performance a course of higher education requires. This kind of proactive institutional response is needed in order to help a diversity of students to take advantage of one of life's most meaningful opportunities, higher education.

CONCLUSION AND GUIDELINES

We cannot overemphasize the idea of proactivity as a cornerstone of any effort to keep and sustain students in higher or post-secondary education. It is our belief, well founded in our professional experience, that too many retention programmes are reactive. They wait for a student to experience a serious crisis before the programme is triggered. The student's personal distress escalates and, as a consequence, his or her personal function plummets.

A proactive approach to retention requires educational institutions to use all the information and surveillance systems at their disposal without intruding into the personal sphere of students or acting without their consent. A proactive system of retention reaches out to students, staff and groups to make as many individuals as possible aware of the aims of retention and the availability of programmatic alternatives that students can incorporate into their academic lives to facilitate their success. The proactive features of retention operate to reach out to students whose problems are detected early in their academic careers and who receive a dignified, timely and caring response to these issues. Students can easily trigger the proactive retention effort with little if any anxiety about stigma, discrimination or reprisal on the part of the institution and its members of staff.

The developmental nature of retention can further articulate what proactivity means in practice. A developmental approach to advice and counselling helps students to establish and sustain key relationships with people who can act swiftly and considerately in the resolution of student-defined issues. These relationships are strong enough to support frequent-enough contact so that student situations are monitored, thus facilitating quick action to resolve issues. Advisors express an interest in the 'whole' student, who is seen as an effective agent in the mastery of the student role. Thus, advisors do not merely help schedule classes and identify required courses but rather they facilitate student development, which expresses itself in:

- a student's growing awareness of educational options;
- an understanding of institutional expectations;
- the mastery of the student role;
- the students' sense of ownership over their own educational experience;
- a transformation of self as evidenced by a growing self-confidence and the achievement of tangible academic success in the role of student.

So perhaps we can begin to view institutional efforts to keep students in higher education as a proactive set of actions that together facilitate the development of students who are learning how to perform in new settings and with new sets of expectations. Many people working in higher education may want students to come prepared to be students who require little support in their mastery and achievement of what educators expect of them. However, even the most talented students may benefit from a proactive response to their development and to the provision of support designed to help them master the role of student in whatever setting or at whatever level they find themselves.

Part III

Five dimensions of retention programmes

7

Dimension 1: The scope of the retention programme

MAIN POINTS OF THE CHAPTER

- In this chapter, scope refers to the number of retention assets the educational institution will incorporate to keep students in higher education.
- The scope of retention reflects the institution's conception of how it will develop its students.
- The scope of the retention programme brings student development alive by addressing student readiness and self-understanding, academic development, personal development, and professional and career development.
- Retention is a change process that requires students to make a commitment to the mastery of the student role. The retention programme may need to help students to engage in their own preparation to stay in higher education. This preparation process refers to the development of readiness.
- Those students who are not prepared for higher education may experience considerable distress and anxiety. It is the role of the retention programme to anticipate this stress and to assist students to manage it so they can move ahead in their educational pursuits.
- The development of readiness can be integrated into core courses that assist students to become aware of the requirements of higher education and the opportunities it offers while they develop core academic skills or competencies.
- Academic development does not merely require students to acquire core academic skills but also to grasp what is expected of them in institutionally defined roles as students.

- The identification of core academic competencies and their integration into foundation courses can facilitate the academic development of students.
- Some students will benefit from purposeful efforts to assist them to develop personally and socially. Retention may be a product of a growing awareness of self and how higher education can help in the achievement of personal goals.
- Retention programmes may facilitate the vocational identity and maturity of students in preparation for the integration of academic and career interests.
- A focus on vocational, professional and career development may help some students to understand and meet the academic expectations higher education places on them.

The scope of the retention programme reflects how an institution of post-secondary or higher education thinks about the assistance it is willing to offer its students to stay in their courses of study and to achieve success, as either the course or student defines it. We can think of 'scope' as the number of potential retention assets the educational institution incorporates to promote the retention of its students. Retention programmes of narrow scope will not factor in many of these potential assets, perhaps focusing the programme only on the academic issues students may experience in post-secondary and higher education. A retention programme of broad scope will cover a number of factors and attempt to integrate these into a package of services and supports that helps students to master their educational experience in a proactive manner.

It is up to the institution of post-secondary or higher education to decide the scope of a retention effort. Certainly the purpose of this chapter is not to dictate or prescribe this scope. To offer a starting point, we identify four considerations that, taken together, form the scope of the retention programme.

The substantive focus of the retention programme incorporates: 1) student readiness and self-understanding; 2) academic development (the most traditional form of retention programme); 3) personal and social development; and 4) professional and career development. The last two are perhaps the most non-traditional aspects of retention.

A retention programme of broad scope will probably incorporate all four of these. It will offer students experiences, opportunities and supports that assist them to achieve retention through the development of readiness, academic competencies, personal and social awareness, and professional and career awareness and choice.

The idea of development is crucial here in that it focuses the attention of retention leaders on the necessity of helping students to master the role of student in higher education in several different areas rather than equating success in higher education with academic achievement alone. Thus, retention programmes of broad scope are by definition developmental ones. They help students to improve their chances of moving through higher education successfully by paying attention to students' full development as young people who are making the transition into adulthood. And they help students to become more mature so that they recognize the value of higher education to their own aims, and can make use of the resources the educational institution offers to advance their personal, career and academic aims.

READINESS AND SELF-UNDERSTANDING

Any change process requires people to contemplate their readiness to engage in change and to begin to make the preparations to become ready to make these changes. Retention is a change process that requires students to reflect on their preparation to make the changes they need in order to become successful in what they may find to be a new experience and for which they may not be totally prepared.

It is not unusual for institutions to offer experiences that help students to prepare for the changes that participation in post-secondary or higher education demands of them. These experiences may help students to become *aware* of the institution, its requirements and expectations, and its culture. And these experiences may help students to obtain and use *accommodations* that are essential to their subsequent performance in their course of study.

Many students may come to the institution of post-secondary or higher education fully aware of these requirements and expectations, and ready to make those accommodations that are essential to their integration into the educational culture. These students may have considerable tangible and intangible educational assets. For example, their tangible educational assets may include adequate or strong academic grades as well as adequate or strong academic skills and competencies. Their intangible educational assets may include awareness of educational expectations and requirements. They may possess insight into the educational culture gained from anticipatory guidance offered by parents, teachers and other people who are keenly aware of what the academic setting requires. In terms of self-understanding, these students may have clearly identified aspirations and aims that they have developed from their own life experiences, exposure to mentors and guidance from family members. So they are 'ready' to engage in post-secondary or higher education, and they can handle (although perhaps with some initial stress) what the institution requires of them.

Those students who are not ready to engage in the educational setting may require enhanced opportunities to become aware of their setting and to make the

113

accommodations that they need to make. Some students are not fully prepared for higher education, and they may find themselves anxious and distressed about entering the institution and embarking on their academic work. This readiness is not merely academic in nature. It may be driven more by self-concept and identity relating to why they are enrolled in post-secondary or higher education, and what will animate their performance and support their persistence. These students may not have strong educational self-concepts and identities. Their own understanding of what post-secondary or higher education means to them and how they are going to use it may not be well developed, resulting in the absence of an essential maturity required for effective performance in their academic career.

This is not the student's problem alone. It is an institution's responsibility to foster readiness and self-understanding by making it a natural part of the educational experience. Thus, readiness becomes an important feature of any retention programme.

How institutions are fostering readiness

There is no one way to address readiness. In the United States, undergraduate courses are increasingly using the first two terms as periods in which to socialize students into the culture of post-secondary or higher education. Institutions are fashioning and offering special courses that integrate opportunities to develop core academic competencies with activities that help students to become aware of their new roles, and how to make successful accommodations in the new culture. Ordinary members of the teaching staff may teach these courses, the kind students will experience in their academic courses, or they may be taught by combinations of teaching staff and student development staff. These courses may also offer a strong group component that helps students to get to know their peers and to develop strong relationships, an important feature of readiness since many students may come to the institution with few if any established relationships with other students.

The institutions creating these courses recognize that students should not be thrown into higher education without some preparation and readiness, a recognition that is not merely confined to undergraduate education. Even post-graduate courses of study recognize the importance of readiness especially by helping students to gain an initial understanding of professional roles so that their subsequent educational experience can make more sense to them as they progress through it. Three examples of this readiness development are as follows:

● There are law schools that offer intensive courses in the 'profession of law' during the first term. These courses integrate basic legal theory, legal research and legal writing with issues pertaining to the practice of law so that students understand what lawyers do and how they function from a practice perspective. These small courses may serve as a refuge for students from large lecture courses, allow them to interact intensively with a member of staff and offer them opportunities to get to know their peers as aspiring lawyers.

● There are medical schools that help students to survey the medical profession early in their educational careers, and to gain an early understanding of the practice of medicine as they begin their intensive progression through basic science and clinical education. Some medical schools offer concentrated modules in the first term that help students to become aware of key educational and professional values such as ethics, research-based practice and outcome-based medical care.

● There are colleges of social work and nursing that offer 'practice labs' before students enter their fieldwork or traineeships. These labs help students to gain and refine core practice competencies such as empathic responding, relationship formation, interviewing and the helping process. The practice labs are kept small so that group interaction enables students to obtain a considerable amount of practice and feedback. In addition, the labs help members of staff to understand the preparation of their students, and the assistance they need to progress in their career choice as aspiring social workers or nurses.

It is difficult to judge whether students are ready to engage in post-secondary or higher education. Some courses may build readiness right into their curricula and assume that all students will benefit from the development of their readiness. There are undergraduate courses that focus on student awareness of the institution and its educational resources as a standing requirement for all students. The social work and nursing labs, the law school courses on the profession of law and the introductory courses on medical practice outlined in the examples above are part of the standing curricula of these schools and all students move through them as key elements of their academic careers and professional socialization. Integration of readiness into the curriculum has the advantages of not isolating a specific group of students, and it does not induce the stigma that more specialized retention efforts may create for some students.

Other readiness efforts may focus on specific subgroups of students whom the institution of post-secondary or higher education identifies as potentially at risk of failure. The identification of these students may be driven by the use of academic criteria, perhaps secondary school grades in key courses or the use of standardized test scores.

The importance of self-direction to readiness

These measures are insufficient since perhaps the most critical readiness issues pertain to the more intangible considerations discussed earlier in the chapter. The core of readiness involves whether students are able to engage in enough self-direction to persist, perform well and reach those benchmarks or milestones that are essential to their academic progress and success.

The development of readiness involves helping students to understand why they are in higher education, helping them to make explicit their aspirations and aims, and helping them understand what they need to achieve in order to make these aspirations and aims a reality. In other words, readiness relates to helping students to strengthen or expand their identities and self-concepts as students. Students will come into post-secondary or higher education at different levels of readiness, and the institution must recognize this and respond as individually as possible to each student's situation, circumstances and history.

The best readiness approach helps students to prepare themselves to meet the challenges of higher education in a manner that makes sense to them, as they define it. Teaching staff and student development staff may want to inquire into how well students understand themselves as students, and why they have chosen to enter the institution. Even academically strong students may be puzzled by these questions, which illustrates that the most talented student may benefit from a readiness experience. A student-centred approach to readiness and retention suggests that all students can benefit from a menu of readiness opportunities from which to choose, before moving further into their academic careers.

ACADEMIC DEVELOPMENT

Institutions of post-secondary or higher education may consider the academic development of students to be the core aspect of any retention programme. After all, it is academic skills and competencies that influence if not determine success in higher education. Students who do not have at least the core array of academic competencies the institution demands will stand out, and will probably fall behind in their academic careers almost immediately. In addition, the literacy requirements of post-secondary and higher education are accelerating. As societies become more scientific and incorporate advanced technologies, numeracy, computer literacy, and basic understanding and use of the scientific method all become increasingly important. These newer forms of literacy are taking their place alongside the more traditional yet still critical forms of reading, writing and composition, and oral presentation. More specialized forms of literacy emerge in professional courses where human relations skills are increasingly valued, and competencies in the integration of an intellectual and emotional understanding of the world become important requirements in service, helping and teaching careers. Students come into education with different and varying developmental gifts, and it is important for institutions to value them and facilitate their development and expression.

The new forms of literacy in combination with the more traditional forms of academic competence signal the vast changes that are occurring in academic development in post-secondary and higher education. Thus, perhaps the highest form of academic development is the ability to engage in self-directed learning over a lifespan in which careers, work and vocation will continually change.

Identifying values

So how should we look at academic development as an aspect of a proactive programme of retention and student persistence in the light of a changing notion of what constitutes literacy? There are two important questions here that perhaps conflict in practice. One question is normative in character. What does the institution as a representative of a society's commitment to education define as the essential competencies of an educated person? Another question is more idiographic in character. What criteria does a course of study require of its students so they perform their professional or career function in at least an adequately competent manner? These two questions reveal the strain in contemporary post-secondary and higher education. What are the general skills and competencies of graduates? And what are their specialized skills and competencies?

Academic development goes to the core of social values, particularly those values the society embraces and seeks to perpetuate. A traditional university may prioritize a set of values that are different from those of the new university. A professional department in a large research university may prioritize a set of values that differ from those of a smaller post-graduate college with a strong vocational orientation toward education.

So a fundamental issue that pertains to the academic development of students and retention is whether a particular course of study can identify what it values, and translate these values into the core and advanced academic competencies of its students. It is important for the post-secondary or higher education course to make these values explicit. This is crucial so that:

- students know what they need;
- teaching staff and student development staff can identify whether students have or do not have these core competencies or capacities;
- the institution can link students to the appropriate experience to develop what they need in order to move forward in their institutional academic careers.

These three points illustrate how retention is not a student problem. As with readiness, academic development requires students to understand what is expected of them in institutionally defined roles as students and it requires an institutional effort that is responsive to students so that they obtain the assistance they need to meet institutional expectations. Thus, a core aspect of retention lies in what the institution and its representatives expect of students, and in how the institution helps students to meet these expectations successfully.

Expectations and the institution's role: an example

A small liberal arts college located in a major urban centre in the United States prides itself in not only its retention rates but also the high percentage of its students who go on to doctoral and professional post-graduate courses. The mission of the college is to prepare its students for entry into the professions at the post-graduate level and, as a result, it focuses its energy on improving its undergraduate courses. It offers only a selected handful of post-graduate courses. By virtue of its affordability, location and flexibility the college attracts students who may be considered from the perspectives of demographics, age, previous education and race to be 'non-traditional students'. Many of the college's students come with deficits in traditional academic competencies or with special learning needs. Nonetheless, the college has given a great deal of thought to what it means for students to be well educated and prepared for the next steps in higher education. The college expects its students to be able to perform seven core competencies by the end of the first year. These are to:

1. research an issue in the humanities, social, or physical and biological sciences using the physical and automated resources of a college library;
2. prepare an evidence-based research paper using appropriate grammar, style, format and references;
3. describe and illustrate the scientific method in a field of their own choosing;
4. demonstrate computer literacy in the retrieval, use and analysis of information;
5. organize and present an argument orally before an audience of peers;
6. use descriptive statistics in the analysis of a problem;
7. describe in writing their career direction.

These seven competencies do not exhaust the college's commitment to the education of its students but serve as the foundation on which the students' selection of their areas of study and their liberal education are built. Members of the teaching staff share a strong consensus on these seven competencies, and they incorporate them into the core first-year courses, so students have ample opportunities to learn them and how to use them in their academic work. The college is small enough for students who experience difficulty to be identified, and student development staff can offer a prescriptive response to address the students' needs. Students demonstrate their acquisition of these competencies through the preparation of their own portfolios, which are reviewed by tutors when students acquire enough credits to move on in their educational careers beyond the first-year level. There are two major checkpoints for the appraisal of academic development early in the career of students. The demonstration of competencies is integrated into key core courses, and there is a summative appraisal at a milestone point in the careers of students. The college's policy is that students must master these seven competencies before proceeding in their education.

The role of teaching staff

We offer this college as an example of how an institution defines an educated person who can proceed in his or her education, rather than as a model. The example helps us to explicate how important it is for an institution to make known to its students and staff what is expected of an educated person who needs to face a world where technological, social and economic change will proceed unabated for the foreseeable future. The college's explication of these core competencies shows how it cares about the learning of its students, and how these competencies frame the early learning career. It also demonstrates how critical members of the teaching staff are to academic development, and to serving as checkpoints and monitors of this process for each student.

The value of making academic development explicit lends itself to tracking and identifying the needs of students as a natural process of staff–student interaction. Half-way through a first-year sociology course, an instructor found that three students were unable to describe the application of the scientific method to social problems. The instructor knew it was her responsibility to link students to the student development centre where each could get an in-depth tutorial on the scientific method. The students were relieved to have a way of mastering this expectation. An understanding of college expectations made this a student–staff–college collaboration. Teaching staff knew what to look for in terms of student performance and where to refer students if they fell short of this performance. Students had available an opportunity to enhance their performance and to meet the expectation. And the college offered a substantive resource to enable students to meet the expectation.

The enabling function of teaching staff is an important aspect of this college's response to retention. Teaching staff are expected to engage their students around the seven competencies. In the example above, staff re-enter the lives of their students as they near the completion of their modules on the scientific method. Staff review this work to assess whether the competency is fulfilled for the courses they taught. Thus, members of staff fulfil their function not only with regard to the substance of the course, but also with regard to the substance of the competency. The effort on the part of this college is exemplary, and it reflects a principle of retention that programmes of post-secondary or higher education cannot avoid. Members of the teaching staff are indispensable to the achievement of student retention and persistence, particularly in the realm of academic development.

The academic development infrastructure

This example also highlights the academic development capacity of the educational course. It is not enough for teaching staff to identify students' academic development needs. Teaching staff must be able to direct and steer students and, as in the case of the college serving as our example, teaching staff must be able to steer students to substantive services that offer them assistance to address the competencies they must acquire.

This academic development infrastructure may exist in centralized locations of the institution, or it may be decentralized in sub-academic locations such as in departments, or it may be so decentralized that members of the teaching staff themselves work directly with student advisees whom they assist to meet academic expectations. In the latter case, advice and counselling become a part of the formal teaching responsibilities of each member of staff.

Of particular importance is that the academic development options available to students are accessible and responsive to them. The academic unit should not communicate to students that it is unwilling to help them to develop through programmes that respond to their needs and to their development.

The outcome perspective

Finally, the academic unit must consider academic development from an outcome perspective. Some academic units may simply define outcome as testing. Students are required to achieve appropriate test scores in areas that are important to academic performance. Thus, tests are used to appraise proficiency in the areas of algebra and higher forms of mathematics, language or writing. Other academic units frame outcome from the perspective of performance. They want students to be able to achieve the academic expectation of their standing educational course. Outcome here is conceived as the ability to impress teaching staff with a performance that meets the spirit and substance of the academic expectation. Whatever approach the programme uses, what is important is that students are aware of the outcome they must achieve, and that they are judged in terms of whether this outcome is achieved or not. The academic development programme is results-oriented and not merely effort-oriented.

Characteristics of the academic development programme

The academic development programme, therefore, can take many different forms. However, it should embody at least five characteristics:

- The academic unit identifies what it values and translates these values into core or advanced academic expectations.
- Students who do not meet these expectations are identified in a manner that does not stigmatize them but that seeks to help them develop.
- Teaching staff are involved in the identification and monitoring of the academic competencies their students must acquire.
- Students have access to responsive academic development opportunities that help them to address their academic needs.
- Academic development is outcome-based. Thus, the achievement of substantive outcomes enables students to move on in their academic careers and to meet institutionally defined expectations.

PERSONAL AND SOCIAL DEVELOPMENT

Should student retention and persistence programmes pay any attention to the personal and social development of their students? Certainly this is an important question that leaders of such programmes should consider in establishing the scope of student retention and persistence activities. Personal and social development is part of the scope of student retention and persistence programmes for one fundamental reason. Institutions of post-secondary and higher education are more than places where students are educated from an academic perspective. They should consider and act on the full development of their students and offer them ways to understand and appraise themselves other than on academic criteria alone.

Students often learn about themselves and their social world through their participation in higher education. The academic aspect is an essential feature of an education, but students also have opportunities to broaden their personal and social world of education, and broaden their perspectives of themselves by the sheer number of opportunities, activities and resources post-secondary or higher education can bring to them.

Students of modest academic performance grow and develop during these essential years when the learning of childhood and adolescence coalesces with the accelerated learning of young adulthood. It may be a disservice to students to focus on their academic development alone without giving them other sources of hope and reference by which to judge themselves as efficacious human beings. The institution of post-secondary or higher education, at all levels, brings students into contact with other people, social events and activities, and cultural events.

Many students do not have strong academic interests, yet discover or acquire other interests or skills. These may be life skills that can play important roles in the students' future lives as citizens, workers and family members. It is very difficult to predict life success, but it should not be confined to academic criteria alone.

The institution's role in personal and social development

Thus an important aspect of retention and persistence may come in the form of the investments post-secondary and higher educational courses make in the personal and social lives of students. This may be the time when students fashion a vision about the life direction they want to take. Students may form essential partnerships or they may discover themselves culturally or politically through events or courses in the institution or through group affiliations.

What are the implications for student retention and persistence? Students may benefit from opportunities to discover themselves. This does not mean that students are merely encouraged to get involved in formal activities, but are encouraged to cherish opportunities that reveal who they are, what they want to become or what they could become. Probably too few institutions help students to discover the nuances of college life by showing them the artistic, cultural, scientific, occupational and social opportunities that abound in most educational settings. It is beneficial to help students find a match between who they are, what they want to try out and what the campus has to offer that can help them to answer some of their personal questions about direction and aims.

Community service education is growing among students around the world, not merely as an alternative to a strict academic routine, but as an option that offers students opportunities to learn about themselves through service. Some students use community service education as an opportunity to further their readiness for a career or profession, but it may also help them identify their values and interests, and make choices about what they like or dislike.

Thus, 'community service education' may serve not only the community, but the personal development of students, as well. Critical decisions may come out of these educational options. They are critical because they help shape the perspectives students hold of themselves, which in turn can influence the choice of academic course and career direction. Some students may learn substantive skills that reinforce a view about who they are and what they value. For example, students in a Central American agricultural station engage in community development projects of their own design. They work in small groups with staff mentors who help them to address the economic and political obstacles to their projects. The group design of the projects is key because each student receives abundant feedback from his or her peers about performance, work style and achievements. The students form an identity within their group, and learn about themselves as community developers. The personal growth that each student achieves is based on both technical and social aspects of the projects. The staff members emphasize that they are not merely training technicians but developing 'self-aware' community practitioners.

One student persisted to a bachelor degree because he loved theatre, although he did not understand what this meant for his academic career and professional direction. He persisted through some dark times, but the retention programme was a bright light. His counsellor was committed to helping him to learn about himself personally, emotionally and socially through theatre.

He found the core requirement part of his course difficult, and did not enjoy it, but he loved his main subject, which was the performing arts. The university performing arts programme was his refuge, and he sank a considerable amount of personal time in volunteer activity. Over two years he learnt about every major function and aspect of a community theatre.

In the end, he failed as an actor, screenwriter and set designer, but teaching staff were very supportive and kept saying to him that with his enthusiasm he would discover his vocation in the arts. His peers always complimented him for his devotion to the arts. He graduated with a bachelor's degree in fine arts, and went on to work in a community arts programme where he became quite effective as the company's resource and fund-raising specialist. This became his calling.

After five years of this work he won admission into a Master's course in nonprofit management where he refined his skills in fund-raising. Now he is effective in donor prospecting, relationship development with donors and social marketing. He has a thorough grounding in the arts that equips him with the ability to interpret the needs of the theatre to potential donors. He says that without the personal development in the last two years of his undergraduate course when staff, peers and other volunteers encouraged his personal journey in the arts he would never have discovered himself.

This example is illustrative of a calling, and is perhaps unusual and not relevant to all students. But it does show that there may be a calling in many students, and that the years spent in post-secondary and higher education is a time of preparation, self-discovery and personal exploration. It is time well spent and can foster positive transitions into adult life.

A retention and persistence programme can lay the foundation of this self-discovery. It can communicate to students that the institution values personal discovery and the effort students make to discover themselves. It can help students to organize this experimentation, helping them to link to alternative learning experiences, and to evaluate the impact of these experiences on their interests, values and aims. It can help students to make use of this self-knowledge in the choice of formal academic courses and in the selection of academic subjects. This aspect of the scope of the retention programme is critical because it can help students to identify why they are involved in post-secondary or higher education.

VOCATIONAL, PROFESSIONAL AND CAREER DEVELOPMENT

Many students consider this aspect of a retention and persistence programme to be the 'bread and butter' of post-secondary or higher education. Gone are the days when a liberal education was an end in itself. Even students who are interested in a general, liberal or interdisciplinary education want to prepare for the world of vocation, profession and career. Given the social dynamics of work and the changes likely in the near and distant future, most students think often about the world of work and the direction they may want to take. Another point is the expense of contemporary post-secondary and higher education, which has accelerated over the past three decades. Why do so many people enter higher education, and why are members of minority groups so eager to invest precious scarce resources in the pursuit of higher education? The answer is that, although the cost of higher education has accelerated over the years, the economic benefits it produces have grown at a far higher rate. Post-secondary and higher education is a sound investment in one's future.

Retention and persistence programmes need to recognize that students come into post-secondary and higher education perhaps more with vocation, profession and career in mind than academic matters. The academic context is a means to an end, and perhaps the greatest end for many students lies in where they want to go in the near future. Unfortunately, many students do not have mature notions of what this end is and what it means to them. They may not have any settled understanding of where they think they want to go. They may be unaware of what options they can pursue if they discover that the choice they made at an earlier stage no longer applies.

Students may need to juggle several different conceptions of gainful work and employment, namely vocation, profession and career. They take on new meaning in contemporary post-industrial, industrial and developing economies. The 'one life, one job' mandate and the 'one life, one employer' expectations of previous generations no longer hold true. The age of the portable vocation, profession and career is here, and it appears to be here to stay.

Many students are already involved in work when they enrol in post-secondary or higher education, but it is probably not the kind of work that will suit them for the long term. Many students come to higher and post-secondary education with aspirations for bettering their circumstances. Their parents, siblings, friends and community leaders suggest new directions and expectations. They point to higher education as a place to achieve more and to become prepared for increasingly competitive employment markets.

The idea of vocation suggests suitability for a particular kind of work. It involves a match between a job and what a student can do or learn to do. The technical idea of vocation contrasts with the social idea of a profession in which society legimates and protects a certain role and function largely through a demanding course of post-secondary education and post-graduate training. The idea of a career perhaps relates to both vocation and profession. A career asks for the commitment of students to an endeavour that extends into the future and requires a progressive and continuous development of vocationally and professionally relevant skills. Of course, the heightened pace of social change expresses itself in both career development and career change. Students can find that the career for which they prepare leads them to other career choices and opportunities, a situation that now raises and will continue to raise the importance of life-long, self-directed learning and personal development.

The institution's role in vocational, career and professional development

Vocational, career and professional development as aspects of programmes of student retention and persistence may be increasingly important as social and technological changes induce new expectations about work performance, productivity and effectiveness. The introduction of these aspects into retention and persistence underscores the importance to students of their vocational, professional and career self-concepts and identities. By revealing these to students, it can make their academic pursuits more relevant and clarify to them why certain knowledge bases, skill sets and competencies are important to their success in the world of work.

Vocational development may actually come first in a programme of student retention and persistence. Vocational development raises questions about a student's basic vocational identity and maturity. What do students know about the world of work? What are their basic work values? What knowledge, skills and competencies have they gained from the work they have engaged in as child, adolescent and young adult? What interests, skills and abilities do they bring to the world of work and how do these fit with their perspective of what kind of work they want to pursue in adult life?

Responding to these questions may require the retention and persistence programme to offer interest, aptitude and competency testing to students who want to explore their vocational sense of self and their identities. Formal testing can offer students ways of looking at themselves and reflecting on who they are or who they want to be in the world of work, but counselling on an individual or group basis in which students can clarify what they learn about themselves and its academic and personal implications should augment this testing. Such interpretative work can open the eyes of some students and suggest that they are embracing inaccurate expectations about themselves and what they want to achieve in post-secondary or higher education.

This interpretative work may also create some personal conflict for those students who realize that their selection of a particular vocation may be more a product of family, parental or cultural expectations than a product of their own aspirations. Thus, counselling may help students identify these issues and help them resolve the issues before they find themselves pressured by family expectations to enter a particular field.

Students preparing for teaching may find that they are really more interested in sales and marketing. This revelation, clarified through testing and counselling, may help them understand why their motivation to achieve passing grades in a teacher preparation course faltered.

Vocational development work may be supplemented by learning directly about various vocational opportunities. It can help students to demystify their choices, and help them come to grips with the performance expectations a particular kind of vocation demands of students. Vocational development work can be carried out in conjunction with co-operative education, brief trial work projects and work-study options. It can help students to build bridges between the world of work and the world of academic preparation.

The student retention and persistence programme can move further into the world of work by focusing on professional and career development. Here students can explore major professions or careers, and clarify the academic and preparation demands each kind of profession creates for its aspirants. A student preparing for the profession of engineering may shadow an engineer for a brief period of time. The student can observe the work directly and find out how academic skills and competencies come into play in an engineering work setting. Students in a pre-engineering curriculum can examine the core academic competencies this plan of study requires and identify how a practising engineer uses these competencies. Observation of and interviews with an engineer can offer data that students can integrate into reflective papers on what engineering involves and how it fits the preferences of the student. The integration of the world of work and academic work can facilitate students' own appraisal of their fit with the profession they contemplate entering.

Students exploring a particular profession may find that over the long term a career in this particular area is not appropriate for them. They may discover aspects of work conditions, salary and performance requirements that do not fit what they dream about or value. Although the profession looks good from the outside, students may find that many practitioners leave the profession within the first five years, suggesting to them that they may want to explore other options.

More extended opportunities for experiencing a profession can be incorporated into this aspect of the student retention and persistence programme. Traineeships and independent studies can be used as vehicles to help students to explore, experience, try and evaluate different aspects of a profession. As with vocational development, when these kinds of experiences are linked to counselling, students can reflect on what they are learning about themselves and their choice about profession. This counselling can help students to become aware of academic requirements and expectations about academic performance. Students can then identify action steps to address academic inadequacies using the academic expectations of the profession they seek to enter as the yardstick of their performance.

The purpose of incorporating vocational, professional and career development into the scope of the retention and persistence programme is to give meaning to the academic requirements and expectations students must fulfil. Integrating work and academic experience can offer students more reference points about their life options, and link the present to the future, fostering a life-planning or career-planning approach to the education of students who may not persist without a tangible goal in mind. This kind of stimulus may be just what some students need to persist in post-secondary or higher education. Supplemented with an active agenda of advice and counselling students can sort out the direction they want to take and the requirements they must meet in the academic world to make their aspirations a reality.

CONCLUSION AND GUIDELINES

This chapter continued the theme of student development by offering more conceptual depth to this important but very complex idea. Students can grow in many ways, and they can acquire more insight and understanding into themselves academically, personally, socially and vocationally. Thus, student development has much to do with the maturation of students as they confront issues their education provokes, resolve these issues and come to know themselves as individuals with numerous dimensions. The academic sphere may be only one aspect of this growing sense of self, and even within the academic sphere students may differ tremendously in academic interests and gifts.

The scope of the retention programme can take advantage of these dimensions or focuses. Students may find meaning in social involvement, academic mastery or the establishment of a vocation or career. A student's discovery of meaning may be the most important outcome of any retention programme. Indeed, perhaps the most proactive retention programme will help students to contemplate their own meaning and stake out the aims they must pursue and realize to make this meaning a reality.

The discovery of meaning and the achievement of those expectations a course requires of students may be the basis of the maturity students need in order to persist in the world of higher education. With such maturity students can master what might once have appeared to be insurmountable issues. A retention programme of broad scope may help students who were once at risk to make sense of their circumstances and make a commitment to their education. This commitment and its execution are the fundamental elements of retention or persistence.

8

Dimension 2: Sponsorship of the retention programme

MAIN POINTS OF THE CHAPTER

- The aim of sponsorship is to place the retention programme in a viable context or set of circumstances.
- This chapter incorporates three approaches to sponsorship: collaborative sponsorship between groups outside and inside the campus, external sponsorship by a community group, and internal sponsorship.
- Sponsorship involves intra-organizational and inter-organizational arrangements to make a retention programme a reality in the institution.
- A collaborative approach to sponsorship enables two or more institutions or groups to combine resources useful to the implementation of a retention programme.
- Collaborative approaches typically help a retention programme to specialize by focusing on a specific population of students or on a specific issue.
- Some external institutions or groups may create their own retention programme to address the needs of their clients who are students on a variety of post-secondary or higher education courses.
- Internal retention programmes typically lie within a matrix of decentralized and centralized services that together form the university or college retention effort.

There are numerous choices that retention leaders can make concerning the establishment of a retention programme in an educational community. In this chapter, we ponder the options that are available in the sponsorship of the retention programme. Sponsorship involves the critical decisions and efforts programme and administrative leadership take to place the retention programme within a viable context or set of circumstances. We examine the implications of collaborative sponsorship between internal and external entities, external sponsorship when a community organization seeks to promote retention, and internal sponsorship of the retention programme. Sponsorship does indeed involve intra-organizational and inter-organizational linkages that the retention programme requires so it can carry out effectively an institutional or organizational mission of keeping students in higher or post-secondary education.

THE SPONSORSHIP OF THE RETENTION PROGRAMME

It is important to differentiate the sponsorship of a retention programme from the endorsement of such a programme. Many institutions of post-secondary or higher education would endorse the importance of retention, particularly in the current environment of the expansion of educational options and the explosion of competition for students., As we emphasized in previous chapters, educational courses of study at different levels (eg undergraduate and post-graduate) are attempting to keep their students persisting in their academic careers. Formulating a retention mission is certainly one of the most important acts of endorsement an institution can make, but once this endorsement is made it opens up basic questions about what entity either within or outside the institution will take responsibility for a retention programme. Sponsorship of the retention programme can come from many different sources.

COLLABORATIVE RETENTION PROGRAMMES BETWEEN HIGHER OR POST-SECONDARY EDUCATION AND COMMUNITY AGENCIES

Sponsorship is an important aspect of establishing the retention programme because it can be handled in different ways, which may have different consequences for the salience and viability of the programme. A collaborative approach to sponsorship enables two or more institutions to combine resources, personnel and competencies perhaps to target specific populations and assist members of these populations to achieve certain academic outcomes. From our own research we have discovered a number of different examples of shared sponsorship, such as:

129

- a women's advocacy centre located in a large urban area, which works with three local colleges to co-sponsor retention and academic support schemes for women returning to higher education after divorce;
- a social service agency working with a small university to facilitate the success of women moving from dependence on state benefits to employment and subsequently to a profession;
- a large professional association working with a polytechnic institute to facilitate the academic success of students who come to the polytechnic without a strong technical background in basic sciences.

Voluntary and social service organizations combining their special interests in students with certain backgrounds or experiences with the academic retention resources of an educational institution is a powerful model of collaboration. Each organization can bring something unique to the enterprise. For example, the social service agency with a commitment to helping women escape poverty probably understands the social problem women in this situation face, and has expertise in organizing those resources they need to integrate education into their family and work life. The agency probably lacks expertise in helping women experiencing poverty to gain the basic academic competencies they need to enter higher or post-secondary education, to organize the financial assistance they need and to help them navigate the culture of higher education. These competencies belong to the institution of higher education, but the institution may not be sensitive to organizing the supports that will help women coping with poverty to move successfully into student roles.

Collaborative or joint sponsorship of retention programmes will enable both community organizations and institutions of higher or post-secondary education to focus their efforts on the needs of specific populations. They can then develop specialized focuses to institutional retention programmes, for example:

- supported education programmes that help students with disabilities to sustain themselves in student roles;
- transitional educational programmes designed to help students to organize community living resources and educational support resources for a limited period of time as they move into the status of student;
- mentor-based educational programmes designed to augment the emotional and academic support of students who are seeking success in specific educational curricula such as engineering, the sciences or teaching.

Some of our colleagues criticize these collaborative efforts on a number of scores. They note that institutions of higher education are not willing to collaborate with relatively small community organizations and agencies, and that it is difficult for these agencies to get institutions of higher education to act with a shared sense of passion for the specific populations the agencies represent within the community. People with serious mental illness, members of minority populations and people coping with poverty are probably marginalized in the general community, and their relatively unempowered situations may not help them to be heard on university or college campuses. In addition, these colleagues suggest that collaborative or jointly sponsored efforts will fragment unnecessarily any retention programme. In other words, rather than having a unified retention programme targeted on those students who are not doing well, a college's retention programme will be split among several different groups.

We do not agree with these criticisms. It is possible for a college or university to have a core retention programme from which different or more specialized retention resources are articulated. There is no reason, as we saw in Chapter 1 with Charlie, why students with serious mental illness cannot participate in a common orientation, academic enrichment and academic support programme while they get more specialized services from community-based personnel situated outside the institution or co-located with other student development staff inside the institution.

Features of a successful collaborative approach

We have witnessed situations where some colleges are not responsive to community agencies or student advocates from professional or voluntary associations. We have also seen colleges or universities that have been quite sensitive and responsive to external requests for collaboration. We find that success stories of collaboration have certain features. The leadership of the institution of higher or post-secondary education endorses the legitimacy of community groups and recognizes the importance of working closely with them. It is likely that the institution has a strong community relations team, which is up to date on alternative approaches to community–institution partnerships and which interacts with the representatives of a number of different educationally marginalized groups. The institution's own retention mission recognizes the variation in retention needs and challenges members of different groups face. It is likely that members of these groups participated in the formation of this mission, making inter-organizational understanding a product of the early planning of the retention effort.

We have found that successful community–institution collaboration requires community agencies and groups to be sensitive to the educational institution. They understand the culture of higher education and the countervailing expectations these institutions must grapple with in making retention a viable aspect of college life. Effective community agencies do not rigidly demand the commitment of resources to their ideas. They do not demand that the institution prioritize the groups they represent over other groups. These agencies understand that resources are scarce and, if they can bring to the collaboration specific assets that can extend the retention competencies of the educational institution, then they will be more successful than those agencies that do not come with anything in hand.

Success of these collaborative retention programmes can also be a product of the emerging diversity of most institutions. Voluntary associations in the community can link with student associations, while those agencies seeking to advocate for specific student groups can find collaborative involvement with a student association that represents such students in the institution. The joint enterprise of a retention programme, particularly a more specialized one, becomes powerful when it unites several groups such as a community agency, student association group and academic course. We do not view this as programmatic fragmentation. It recognizes that there will be diverse retention efforts linked to core retention programmes and organized under the banner of the institution's retention mission.

The collaborative arrangements of the retention programme can prove to be an effective resource in the marketing of the programme. Joint Web sites may emerge that articulate the integration or co-location of resources with links to academic resources, resources available through student or professional associations, and resources available through community agencies and voluntary ethnic associations. Electronic and print media can identify various contact people within both the university and the community, giving a diversity of options to students who are seeking help or a diversity of options for on- or off-campus referral sources.

The current policy environment favours collaborative arrangements that create synergies achieved through bringing together the distinctive resources of several institutions sharing a joint mission. Collaboration is an aspect of innovation, and the innovation brought by various institutions collaborating to make retention effective for various groups of students can prove to be an asset in the search for funds and resources.

EXTERNAL SPONSORSHIP OF THE RETENTION PROGRAMME

Some community agencies, voluntary associations and professional organizations may find that certain educational institutions are inhospitable toward their overtures for collaboration. Or they may find that higher education is simply unresponsive or unsympathetic towards their retention aims and towards the students they want to serve through retention efforts. An educational institution may consider, for example, that people coping with serious mental illness and seeking to become students are unsuitable for academic involvement and the institution may suggest to the community organization that the organization should go it alone in its efforts to facilitate retention.

The Henderson Agency, a rehabilitation organization devoted to people with serious cognitive disabilities, sought a collaboration with a large university only to find its overtures rejected by the institution. Agency leadership wanted to respond to those rehabilitation clients who were anxious to enter higher education, had a previous background as successful students, but who needed accommodations to the role of student and the learning environment. The university representative noted that the university's office of disability affairs could help make these accommodations on a case-by-case basis. The agency, however, offered a rationale for a free-standing retention programme that the university simply could not or did not want to endorse.

The agency went on by itself to develop within the community a retention programme specifically focusing on the needs of students with cognitive disabilities. The leadership of the agency thought that the programme would serve only the agency's clients but it soon received referrals from the vocational rehabilitation system, other agencies, families and voluntary associations serving people with disabilities.

To expand the programme and the services it offered, the agency established a board composed of representatives of higher education, disability groups, and human and rehabilitation services. The programme soon became an external retention service with links to a range of educational institutions. The Henderson Agency identified best practices in supported higher education in the area of serious mental illness and chose a mentor-based approach. In this approach a mentor would work closely with the student in and outside the institution. Rather than having a free-standing office in a specific institution, the service enabled students to choose their own educational option within the community. The mentor assisted students to organize their own individual strategies for mastering the student role within the educational institution and course of their own choosing.

This case suggests that a community organization or voluntary association is not dependent on a specific institution to create a student retention and persistence programme. What is necessary is that the organization is very clear about what it is trying to achieve through the programme, the purpose of its efforts and the design of the programme. Situating the retention programme outside an institution may be wise when the community agency is seeking to broaden the educational options, venues and types of educational alternatives it offers people who are seeking to become students.

Collaboration in this case will take a different form from the collaboration of an institution of higher education and a community agency seeking jointly to offer a student retention and persistence programme. The external programme may need meeting space in institutions and access to student development, teaching and student affairs staff for participation in its orientation and educational offerings. Some educational institutions will welcome these requests, seeing the efforts of the external programme as a way of building their own student enrolment. Other educational institutions will not be so hospitable and will not readily offer resources to the external programme.

Programme staff will need to be ready for these different responses. The programme itself will need its own mission, identity, leadership, marketing capacity and infrastructure. These resource requirements place a considerable burden on external programmes and help explain why they are difficult to implement and more difficult to sustain unless they are under the sponsorship of an organization that is competent in resource acquisition and development. In addition, the reluctance of some educational institutions to offer resources to the external programme will drive up the cost of the service, which will necessitate even more resource development skill on the part of the external agency.

External retention programmes will probably take root in situations where at least three conditions are fulfilled. First, there are a number of different educational institutions and options within a community, giving potential students a range of choices about higher or post-secondary education. Second, there are potential students whose needs are not met by educational institutions because their needs are too numerous, serious or perceived as lying outside the mission of the educational institution. Third, there is at least one community agency or voluntary association that recognizes the importance of meeting the educational needs of the people it represents and seeks to do so as an act of advocacy. When these three conditions converge the likelihood increases of an external programme emerging within a particular community that is devoted to meeting the academic support and retention of particular groups of students.

INTERNAL SPONSORSHIP OF THE RETENTION PROGRAMME

The sponsorship of the retention programme within an institution of higher or post-secondary education can take many different forms, yet, whatever form this sponsorship does take, we assume that it obtains its direction from a strong institutional endorsement of retention typically through a strong and assertive mission statement.

Perhaps the strongest sponsorship of an internal programme comes from the top, with the programme situated in the office of the senior academic leadership of the institution. The placement of the retention initiative at the highest level of academic governance means that there is the likelihood of the emergence of a policy system that co-ordinates retention throughout the academic institution. In large and diverse institutions, the development and articulation of retention policy becomes very important since this is what will guide the programmatic expression of retention through the institution.

Take, for example, a large research university that offers undergraduate, post-graduate and professional courses of study. The university possesses a large student body, highly specialized teaching staff and a diversity of courses that are disciplinary or interdisciplinary in nature. The educational institution articulates retention as a major policy direction and has created a framework that guides retention throughout the institution. Thus, there is a well-articulated and broadly endorsed student retention and persistence mission. This mission gives direction to the creation of student development programmes and retention services throughout the university under different auspices including the core undergraduate programme, upper-level undergraduate education, pre-professional studies, professional courses and doctoral education. Cutting across these course-based retention efforts are retention support services including academic development, writing workshops, computer literacy, career guidance and development, mental health care and financial aid.

The institutional framework fosters a variety of retention options that form an organizational matrix of decentralized programmes and centralized services. The university attempts to give a unity to this matrix through the structure of the budget. The retention budget brings together various programmes within a framework of retention aims, goals and strategies. All the key players within the university 'retention community' come together half-yearly to fashion a strategic plan that guides the budget and the development and evaluation of retention services and programmes.

This means that the retention practitioner who deals with first-year students is not working in an isolated manner. The practitioners are part of a retention community within the university. They understand the institutional mission, participate in the formulation of retention strategy and work collaboratively with other university staff who devote themselves to retention practice.

There is another aspect to this university's retention programme that is worth noting. Since the overall retention policy is implemented institutionally through a decentralized set of programmes, there is a need for institutional co-ordination of all the activities the retention policy requires for its viability and effectiveness. The university achieves this co-ordination through a retention council whose members are drawn from all over the university community and include retention leadership, teaching staff, student leaders and student development staff. The vice-chancellor appoints the members to this council, and the highest university official responsible for the retention policy chairs it.

The university not only decentralizes retention programmes and services throughout the university but it also seeks to devolve responsibility for retention within academic courses and ultimately into the roles of teaching staff. University policy on teaching excellence reinforces the role of teaching staff in retention activities, the formation of retention initiatives within academic units and degree courses, and innovation in retention practices through the introduction of staff development and funding opportunities. The university identifies the data and information requirements of tracking and monitoring students, and deploys a retention information system that facilitates the flagging of students who may need retention services. The university does not use these data merely to identify students but rather employs them to involve students in a proactive process of mastering the role of student. We outline this process in the next three chapters.

Thus sponsorship within the complex environment of university life can be achieved by centralizing policy, mission, strategy and resources, by decentralizing programmes and services, and by devolving responsibility for retention as a priority of all teaching staff.

CONCLUSION AND GUIDELINES

This chapter has illustrated the importance of sponsorship of the institutional retention programme. The sponsorship offers an opportunity to the institution of post-secondary or higher education to think through the purpose of retention and how it wants to go about the formation, placement and implementation of its retention programmes and discrete services. Collaboration shows that retention may capture the interests and imagination of a number of different groups inside and outside the institution, which underscores the importance of combining and integrating services from a host of different organizations and groups. With the growing importance of higher and post-secondary education in the lives of students around the world, many organizations inside and outside the institution are gaining a stake in the educational persistence and success of their students.

The organization that lies outside the institution of higher or post-secondary education may face numerous challenges and issues as it tries to sponsor a retention programme. Its primary mission may not lie in higher education, but nonetheless it may have an array of supports and resources that are relevant to the facilitation of retention. When its clientele prioritize retention as an important concern, then sponsorship of a retention programme makes sense. Such organizations may find partnerships with other service agencies and with institutions of post-secondary or higher education, but if the organization does not find a hospitable environment for its retention cause, it can consider working as an external agent that seeks to implement its own mission of student retention and persistence. Such an organization will become focused on the people it serves, and other students in the institution may find that this option is not readily available to them.

Sponsorship is indeed a critical feature of any retention effort. Thinking it through as a fundamental dimension will enable a programme to clarify its purpose, direction, services and resources.

9

Dimension 3: The outreach function of the retention programme

MAIN POINTS OF THE CHAPTER

- There are four basic aims of a retention outreach programme: getting the word out among students, teaching staff and other staff; connecting to specific students; facilitating access to the retention programme; and engaging students in the process of retention.
- The message the retention programme deploys about retention will shape how the institution's community comes to know about retention.
- A proactive outreach process will build awareness of the retention programme among important referral sources and users of the programme.
- Connecting to students requires retention programmes to identify relevant students but then programme staff must reach out to these students to foster their understanding of what the retention programme offers.
- Communicating directly with students is important in order to overcome student inaction or their reluctance to make use of retention services.
- Even though retention programmes may take the initiative to link with certain students, it is up to these students to decide whether retention services are relevant to them.
- The site, timing and presentation of retention services influence whether students will make use of them.
- Making retention services informal, supportive and flexible will increase their accessibility to students, particularly those who are reluctant to make use of them.

- The principal outcome of awareness building, connecting and access is the engagement of those students who need retention services.
- Engagement of students involves fostering their commitment to retention and motivating them to get involved in relevant services and supports.

Outreach is one of the most critical dimensions of a programme of retention within higher education. Outreach involves the process of reaching out to those individuals who can identify and refer students who have retention needs as well as reaching out directly to students who have these needs. Effective programmes of outreach do not stay hidden within the institution. Nor should they be inaccessible to students and to those members of the teaching staff, student development staff and members of the community who have a stake in the success of students in higher or post-secondary education. Yet it is likely that programmes of retention do not have infinite resources and must operate within specific complements of resources and budgets.

A well-thought-out outreach initiative can make it possible for each retention programme to identify its objectives for the numbers and types of students it seeks to serve, how to reach out to these students and the scope of effort it seeks to invest in attracting students to the programme. Effective retention programmes cannot be overwhelmed by an excessive number of students, yet, as we noted in previous chapters, the need for retention services may be quite extensive in any given institution. Thus, the outreach initiative must fit into an overall programme strategy that defines and elaborates the principal outcomes the programme seeks to achieve within higher or post-secondary education.

Within this chapter we offer four basic aims of a retention outreach programme. These aims involve:

- *Getting the word out* to those stakeholders who mediate between the student and the retention programme. There are numerous stakeholder groups and it is important for an outreach initiative to focus on the most meaningful ones.
- *Connecting to specific students* who possess the need for retention services in order to help them to understand the programme and assess whether it is useful to them.
- *Facilitating access to the retention programme* in order to optimize its actual use by those students who can benefit from it.
- *Engaging students in the process of retention* so that there is a strong and positive relationship between programme staff and each student they seek to serve.

GETTING THE WORD OUT

'Getting the word out' requires a retention programme to create an image of the programme in the minds of those groups or individuals who are potential users of the programme or referral sources to it. The creation of an image is an act of marketing on the part of the programme and its leadership in which they must identify and describe what the programme seeks to achieve, whom they want to serve and what they can offer to achieve the outcomes the programme defines as important. Refining this image may require the refinement of these attributes through interaction with the members of the principal groups that value the programme and what it can contribute to the success of students. In other words, these groups and individuals can help the programme to refine its message and to establish itself within the community and the institution to ensure that potential users and referral sources learn that it exists and is available to students.

The content of the message is important to helping students become aware of the retention programme in an institution and in subsequently attracting students who have actual or perceived retention needs. A message that emphasizes student deficits and failures may not be an effective way to motivate students to seek out the programme. Although aware of the programme, students may attribute only negative features to it, a process that will probably provoke anxiety. For example, one programme may emphasize in its institution-wide announcements that students who are 'failing to pass courses' should make use of the retention programme. Teaching staff may begin to pay attention to only those students who are failing examinations, failing to follow through on papers or failing to attend class. Of course, students experiencing these kinds of difficulties should probably make their way to the retention programme, but they may do so for the wrong reasons, or they may fail to do so at all because they perceive the programme in a negative light.

Alternatively, a retention programme may frame its services in a positive light, suggesting that it helps students to meet the challenges of higher education successfully. The message may contain a set of criteria that people can evaluate in order to determine whether they should refer someone or, in the case of students, whether they should refer themselves.

This message may have a sympathetic tone, encouraging students who feel overwhelmed by the experience of higher education to make use of the resources of the programme. The programme may over-recruit in this manner but, as part of its outreach initiative, it can subsequently (or eventually) screen in those individuals with the most serious needs such as those students who are failing to pass key examinations or whose enrolment status is jeopardized by course failure. It may also screen out those individuals whose academic needs are not serious but who experience considerable anxiety about their performance. The outreach initiative is responsible for steering those individuals who seek out the retention programme but who are subsequently deemed not to be appropriate. Thus, an objective of 'getting the word out' involves helping each student to achieve a useful disposition through linkage to other institution or community resources.

Getting the word out by developing the image of the retention programme and deploying a positive message regarding its aims may need to cover a broad and diverse set of stakeholders both inside and outside the institution. A general campaign may be undertaken in order to get the word out to key members of groups like teaching staff, student organizations and student development and advice services staff.

A retention programme based in a community college in the United States deploys its message through a broad set of activities its staff undertake in the college:

- The programme makes brief presentations to the college senate almost twice a year to ensure that there is a broad-based understanding of its retention efforts.
- Programme staff keep leaders of student organizations aware of what it offers to students and how to connect students to the programme.
- Programme staff attend the teaching staff meetings of academic units such as departments or divisions within the college to apprise them of the programme's availability and the specific services it offers.
- Staff make presentations to large classes and lecture courses so that individual students understand the aims of the programme and its availability to individual students.
- The programme is experimenting with e-mail to notify students and teaching staff about the services it offers.
- The programme has its own presence on the school's information system through a Web page that integrates student development and 'student success' resources. The programme also incorporates links to other on-campus and off-campus resources (eg emergency loan information and procedures) and the programme exists as a Web link on most departmental Web pages within the college.

This manner of getting the word out about retention services is a resource-intensive process, which is the downside of a proactive approach. But the upside is that it enables the programme to build awareness of its presence in the institution, an important and necessary outcome of getting the word out. Retention staff do not wait for students to discover the programme by accident or learn about it when they are in jeopardy of dismissal, although this will happen in some cases. Well-timed messages, like those that can be delivered to teaching staff at a crucial time like mid-course examinations, may remind these important referral sources to scan their class lists and reach out to students who can benefit from additional assistance.

Such a process does require teaching staff to be receptive to retention messages, and highlights the critical roles they play in retention. Thus, making sure that they are aware of the retention programme and how to steer students to the programme is another important outcome of getting the word out. Building the awareness of teaching staff of their role in fostering retention can be integrated into staff development events. The power of these messages to teaching staff may be strengthened when an institution's own retention mission underscores the critical role teaching staff serve in keeping students in higher education.

CONNECTING TO STUDENTS

Increasingly institutions of higher or post-secondary education are using enrolment and other student databases to identify students who have retention needs. In addition, institutions may use these systems to track and monitor the educational experience of students as reflected by indicators pertaining to enrolment patterns, attendance, completion of academic requirements, course completion and performance in examinations. These data systems require staff to input data at the point of instruction, making the systems labour-intensive but rich in their portrayal of how students are progressing based on academic criteria alone. Automated spreadsheets and grading systems offer staff the means to capture these data, and electronic alert systems can flag students in need using threshold criteria.

Perhaps an advantage of these student information systems is that they enable institutions to identify students who may not be performing well and/or who are not progressing in their educational careers. They become powerful tools in the identification of specific students from large student groups or populations. The misuse of these systems lies in the potential breach of student privacy and the depersonalization of the retention process. Although they can serve as an efficient means for the assessment of the retention needs of students, some institutions will use them merely to alert students through impersonal letters about their status and the jeopardy in which they may find themselves academically.

It is critical to incorporate automated systems of student identification, tracking and monitoring into an interpersonal process that offers students a connection with someone who can interpret their situation for them and assist them to assess the circumstances in which they find themselves. Merely alerting students to a problem is not enough, but offering them contact with a real person who can assist them to identify necessary actions and help them to take these actions is fundamental to the realization of effective retention practice.

Reaching out to students: an example

Susan, a retention counsellor at a relatively large university in the mid-western

United States, makes use of an automated student alert system that enables her to flag what she refers to as 'vulnerable' students. They are vulnerable because their background characteristics and academic performance indicators suggest that they are at risk of withdrawing from higher education. Susan found that merely alerting these students through standard form letters was not an effective way to offer them retention services and resources.

She has changed her procedures for connecting to students, which gives a proactive flavour to her retention programme. After she makes use of the student information system to identify relevant students she designs an outreach letter that is warm and engaging. The letter identifies Susan and her role in the university, and it communicates her concern for what the student is probably experiencing in his or her academic and personal life. The letter welcomes the student to make contact with Susan and the retention programme but also indicates in a very positive tone that Susan will follow up with the student at a class or in the student residence hall to have an initial meeting. Susan is purposefully intrusive in her outreach efforts since she has learnt that many students who are experiencing academic challenges in higher education will not follow up with the programme. She balances the potential ethical issues this intrusiveness can create with the benefits of getting to students early in their academic careers in order to help them prevent subsequent problems and seriously negative academic outcomes like dropping out.

Susan is very persistent in her outreach efforts with what she has deemed to be vulnerable students. The letter is a means of initiating contact in order to make a connection with these students. However, her outreach practices require that she actually connects with these students. After making an initial face-to-face contact, she invites the student to an 'invitational conference'. It is at this conference that connecting with a student occurs, when she seeks to cement the commitment of the student to the retention process. At the conference, she gently identifies the academic circumstances that have brought about the contact and then explains the resources the programme can offer to students to change these circumstances for the better. She wants students to assess whether their involvement with the programme will be useful and to make the choice about whether they will be involved.

Thus, she invites students to become involved in the retention effort but leaves it up to them to make the decision. If students decline involvement, Susan feels that there is still achievement of a major outcome. Students are aware of the availability of the programme, and Susan instructs them in how they can trigger the retention services later if they should so desire. The door is left open and never closed, and nor are students coerced into involvement.

Those students who choose to progress in the retention programme work with Susan to further their understanding of their academic, personal and financial circumstances. Susan conducts a brief screen of the barriers students face and the resources that are available to address and reduce or eliminate these barriers. She develops a more in-depth understanding of students' situations as the retention helping process unfolds (see Chapter 11). She seeks a connection with students at this time and knows that this connection, when handled in a gentle, supportive and caring manner, will form the most powerful retention resource, that is, she forms an initial working relationship with students who have come to their own conclusions (even though they may be tentative and somewhat ambivalent) that they want to turn around for the better their current academic situations.

For Susan the idea of 'invitation' is fundamental to outreach. She needs to identify relevant students, reach out to them through sensitive but perhaps intrusive communications and meet them in order to create the initial relationship. From her experience she knows that the process is not always smooth. Students sometimes complain that Susan has violated their privacy, yet even such students might subsequently make contact with her to seek help.

Susan takes some risks, but she is sincere and her style is warm. She knows that the absence of interpersonal contact with students will not lead to retention. She knows that good outreach not only leads to the identification of students but also offers an opportunity to educate students about the availability of the retention programme and what it can offer to the student. And she knows that students may have strong emotional reactions to her reaching out to connect with them.

Susan's experience is that outreach requires that a retention programme should forge a connection with students who are in need of specific resources to continue their involvement in higher education. For Susan, making this connection is a proactive process that requires her to reach out to students rather than expecting students to come to the programme. This is the essence of retention outreach.

FACILITATING STUDENT ACCESS

Retention outreach also requires a programme to facilitate a student's use of retention resources, which is an important feature of the outreach function. Susan's work is an exemplar of how her programme facilitates access to retention services. She goes to the student since she assumes that most students are unaware of what is available, reluctant to find out about what is available and perhaps somewhat anxious about what making use of retention services means to them, their family and their friends. She feels that if she is proactive in her outreach efforts and in her efforts to form initial working relationships with students then she will reduce barriers to students' use of the programme.

Access also involves the timing of retention services. Many programmes offer services when students are in jeopardy or serious circumstances, which probably gives a crisis orientation to the retention programme. Outreach as access challenges a retention programme to position retention services as early as possible in the career of students.

Access: an example

Joseph's retention programme based at a technical college is a good example. As the leader of the programme, Joseph works with student associations, teaching staff, departments and the student advice services staff to build use of the retention programme early in the educational careers of students.

For example, academic staff can steer students to the retention programme before they start their courses. At enrolment, Joseph's staff members invite students who meet retention criteria to an initial conference. Since the retention programme is based in the advice centre of the technical college, students do not have to go to a specialized physical location that may make them feel different, inferior or stigmatized. The retention staff are co-located with other academic counsellors and it is not readily clear to any student what staff are available for retention and what staff are available for other advice. Joseph likes to 'shroud' the retention programme in other academic and student programmes so that it is relatively unobtrusive. The relative invisibility of the programme does not mean that it is difficult for a student to connect to it and trigger its services. Like Susan's proactive efforts at connecting with students, Joseph knows that the programme has to seek out students in a proactive manner. However, he also understands that students should not be singled out as students who are performing poorly.

The hours of availability of the retention programme are another important consideration in making it accessible to students. Joseph knows that confining the hours of the programme to the traditional business day is not an effective way to serve students. He has created a programme that operates in the evening, at weekends and in the holidays. Programme staff are available to students for face-to-face work, for work over the Internet, or through telephone contact.

Another access innovation of Joseph's programme lies in its management structure and the linkage of this management structure to the temporal framework of the programme. Retention staff are organized into small teams and each team is responsible for a specific number of students. Members of a retention team are responsible for marketing, awareness building, student linkage and student support functions for specific academic departments and/or courses. Retention team members must know all the students the team serves so if a student's counsellor is not available another team member can easily step in to serve the student. This means that few students should experience a disruption of retention services because of the unavailability of their assigned counsellor. Students understand that they too are members of a team and can work with so-called auxiliary personnel until their own counsellor returns.

Joseph's programme also incorporates innovative group approaches to serving students. His approach to retention service is to make student opportunities flexible, informal and highly supportive. Group experiences are available at different times such as weekends and evenings. These group experiences integrate educational opportunities about college resources, the introduction of group members to college academic specialists (such as mental health staff) and the opportunity for group members to support and encourage one another. These group events typically are informal social events. Students attending are looking for fellowship, information about college resources and just social involvement.

Joseph sees the centre as a community for students who need to master the student role. He offers membership to students who soon learn that they are not alone in their quest to achieve success in higher education. The membership orientation of the retention centre strengthens its accessibility because of its informality and supportive character.

Joseph does not seek to coddle students, nor to make them dependent. He does understand retention as a challenge some students will face periodically in their educational careers or consistently during the early parts of their careers. Some students will need intensive services, and others will need supportive services. He wants his centre to be accessible to all students who need its services, and part of access is to offer students a range of services from which they can select for themselves those they feel are the most appropriate to their situation.

ENGAGING STUDENTS

The successful engagement of students in the process of retention is the principal and most important outcome of outreach. By building awareness, connecting to students proactively and facilitating access, the retention programme establishes the foundation on which to engage students in an active process of resolving those barriers that frustrate their success in higher or post-secondary education. A good engagement process results in a contract in which students understand what retention requires of them, understand what the retention programme can offer them and commit themselves to the process of retention.

Chapter 11 outlines the helping process that retention requires. As we noted in previous sections, the intensity and scope of retention will vary for students depending on the number and severity of the barriers they experience in higher or post-secondary education. Engagement assists students to get ready for this helping process so that they can realize as much success as possible from it and so that they can maximize their involvement in moving ahead in their educational careers.

We place engagement within the area of outreach since it encompasses the efforts a programme invests to identify and involve students. Engaged students are those who agree to be involved in the process of retention. They contemplate whether their participation is meaningful to them and come to the conclusion that it is important. This positive response suggests that their continued involvement in higher education is important and that they want to continue an educational career.

Contemplation and agreement to become involved in retention lead to commitment. Those students who are engaged in retention commit themselves to an initial plan of action. They work constructively with the retention practitioner to identify their needs and the barriers they face in their educational careers. This identification and assessment activity may not be as elaborate as later activity when the retention helping process unfolds but there is an initial commitment by students to clarifying what direction the retention effort should take. This commitment solidifies involvement and forges a connection between students and the retention practitioner.

As we have noted throughout this book, and earlier in this chapter, effective retention practice requires someone who is available to the student who cares about the student's success in his or her educational career. The contract between the student and the retention practitioner is the basis of this relationship and infuses it with meaning. The contract represents the readiness of the student to move on in the helping process. The student is engaged and ready to take action. This is the natural consequence of a thoughtful process of proactive outreach.

CONCLUSION AND GUIDELINES

Outreach is a pivotal dimension of any retention programme and will contribute considerably to the subsequent success of the programme in keeping students in higher education. The four aims of the outreach function indicate that the programme works broadly to get the word out first of all. It then connects with appropriate students while it facilitates access of these students to the programme and engages them in a process of development that may incorporate a number of different activities depending on the academic, career and personal needs of students.

The outcomes of outreach are important to consider here. 'Getting the word out' should produce a *general awareness* in the community of higher or post-secondary education so that key stakeholders know that the programme exists and understand its primary mission of retention. 'Connecting with students' enables the programme to establish *initial working relationships* with students and helps them to decide whether to *become involved* in the programme. The 'facilitation of access' makes the program *easy to use* by students who may experience motivational challenges and who may be concerned about how they are perceived by members of the academic community including other students. And, finally, the 'engagement of students' solidifies their *commitment to retention* and *increases their readiness* to proceed into the helping process, Thus, effective outreach is an important core competency of any retention programme. Outreach enables the programme to move from student identification to student involvement and lays the foundation for subsequent retention activity, effort and outcomes.

10

Dimension 4: Roles of retention facilitators

MAIN POINTS OF THE CHAPTER

- The real work of any retention programme lies in the facilitation of student persistence, success and retention. The retention programme helps by helping one student at a time.
- The facilitation of retention focuses on helping students to understand why they want to be involved in higher education, understand the student role, obtain the supports they need and eliminate the barriers that can undermine their success.
- Helping students to get ready to be successful in post-secondary or higher education can involve counselling, interpreting, the provision of information, guidance and assessment.
- Helping students to muster the supports they need can involve resource development, skill development and mentoring.
- Helping students to overcome or defeat barriers can involve troubleshooting, crisis intervention and advocacy.
- Nine important retention roles are identified. These are counsellor, interpreter and information provider, guide, assessor, resource developer, skill developer, mentor, troubleshooter and crisis intervenor, and advocate.

So far we have established that a retention programme incorporates a broad scope encompassing the development of readiness and self-understanding, and academic, personal, and professional and career development. The retention programme requires a well-thought-out strategy of sponsorship that makes retention visible and important in an institution's environment. We pointed out in Chapter 8 that sponsorship may come in the form of collaboration among many different entities or it may come from external or internal sources that operate on their own in relationship to retention aims. However, even with the most ambitious scope and the most productive sponsorship, a retention programme must engage in a proactive outreach to students and staff alike in order to make people aware of what the programme aims to accomplish and how to connect students to the retention effort. A process of proactive outreach may be one of the most important assets of a retention programme and, without it, the retention programme will not have much viability either outside or inside the institution.

Scope, sponsorship and outreach make the retention programme ready for its work. But the real work of retention lies in its facilitation. This chapter looks at the various roles retention facilitators play in any retention programme. We identify a handful of these roles only to highlight how the facilitation of retention operates, but this identification is not exhaustive since there are probably unlimited options. The roles we do identify come from our own experience as social workers practising in higher education. To clarify the importance of facilitation we first examine this idea and then move on to highlight nine roles that facilitators often combine to make the facilitation of retention happen and bring about retention outcomes. We highlight these roles in anticipation of the next chapter where we outline the helping process of retention. Thus, this chapter combines with the next to explicate how retention outcomes are brought about. This process may appear complex but after all retention is complex since it involves a number of different social forces both inside and outside the institution that effective retention programmes must address in order to attain the outcome of keeping students in higher education.

FACILITATION

If we start with the dictionary definition, facilitation comes down to 'making things easier for someone'. As noted in earlier chapters, 'making retention easier' requires at least three things. First, the retention programme must help students to understand why they want to be involved in higher education and to understand the student role, which they must master in order to be successful.

Next, the retention programme must offer substantive supports to students to help them to master the role of student. We suggest a retention programme of broad scope that is very developmental in its orientation. We highlight the importance of helping students to get ready to be successful and to reach a level of self-understanding that fosters the relevance of higher education to them. We then stress the importance of a retention programme helping students to develop academically, personally and professionally. In other words, the retention programme helps students to mature as students and into the role of students.

Finally, the retention programme must help students to overcome, sidestep, manoeuvre or disrupt those barriers that can defeat them, frustrate them or cause them to stop their educational involvement. The idea of persistence links to the reduction of barriers. Students persist as they successfully overcome these barriers. They probably stop persisting when they fail to deal with a barrier. As we identified in an earlier chapter, barriers come in different forms. Many are environmental, however, and come in the form of financial, family and personal issues that, operating singly or in tandem, can be powerful forces in defeating any student.

Facilitation means that the retention programme brings together the ability to foster readiness, offer support and defeat barriers into helping roles within the framework of the programme. These roles incorporate behaviours of people who are expected to help students to achieve retention and persist in their educational careers by mastering the role of student.

In this chapter, we organize facilitation roles by the framework presented above. Some roles are useful in the facilitation of readiness and self-understanding while other roles are useful in mustering support or defeating or overcoming barriers. Here is a way of thinking about these roles:

- Developing readiness through the roles of:
    - counsellor;
    - interpreter and information provider;
    - guide;
    - assessor.
- Mustering support through the roles of:
    - resource developer;
    - skill developer;
    - mentor.
- Overcoming or defeating barriers through the roles of:
    - troubleshooter and crisis intervenor;
    - advocate.

ROLES RELEVANT TO THE FACILITATION OF READINESS

Many educators are aware of the role of counselling and recognize its importance to working with students in higher or post-secondary education. We do not use 'counselling' in this context to mean the process of exploring with students their personal problems and concerns but rather the process of helping students in higher or post-secondary education to clarify their involvement in education and helping them to clarify their strengths and needs in relationship to mastering the role of student. The *counsellor* is concerned with the readiness of students and in helping students to understand the choice they have made to enter higher education.

The counsellor may help students to clarify the importance of higher education to them personally and in relationship to their hopes, dreams and values. Additionally, the counsellor may help students to take a hard look at their personal circumstances and situations and how they want to modify these to accommodate their commitment to higher or post-secondary education. The counsellor is an attentive, warm and friendly ally who does not want to press his or her own values on to the student. The counsellor is not like the member of the teaching staff who tries to dissuade students from moving forward or discourages their involvement in higher or post-secondary education.

Rather, the counsellor listens closely to students within a structured framework of decision making. Indeed, the counsellor knows that students must understand the realities of their choices and what they face in terms of personal commitment and personal cost. Do students understand this decision? Are they ready to act on it? Do they want to spend some time getting ready in order to prepare themselves further for mastery of the student role in higher or post-secondary education? These questions are critical and preparatory ones. Answering them helps students to move forward anticipating the realities of their decisions and choices.

Students may not be fully prepared to make these decisions or choices. They need additional information to proceed in becoming aware of what higher or post-secondary education demands of students and what mastery of the student role means. So another important facilitation role is that of *interpreter and information provider*. The facilitator becomes an educator informing students about requirements, expectations and norms, on the one hand, and opportunities, services and options, on the other hand.

Many students, particularly those without a clear role model for success in higher or post-secondary education, can benefit from an augmented information base and the interpretation of this information to them personally. For example, a student might start an undergraduate science course with the expectation of proceeding to veterinary medicine but without a clear sense of what an undergraduate curriculum will require of him. The facilitator is ready to offer this student relevant information about linking the undergraduate experience to the subsequent professional course and to interpret to him expectations a veterinary course will have of undergraduate performance. The student might say at this point that he is not ready to pursue this career option since he can now interpret his own choices and decisions. The student is successful because he can now interpret his own choices and decisions. The facilitator is successful because he or she has given the student enough information about what to expect and how to perform to clarify aspirations, choices and decisions.

The *guide* may be one of the most important roles by which to facilitate readiness. The guide is willing not only to talk to students and help them to sort out their interests, commitments and decisions but to offer them alternative experiences on which to base their decisions. In a readiness development programme the facilitator guides students through the thicket of campus options, courses and services, helping students to make the experience of higher education less complex. The guide shows students the resources of the institution and takes them through the critical steps needed to become students. Thus, the guide may show students how to apply, how to interact with staff and how to organize a timetable. The guide wants students to become more comfortable with college life through hands-on experiences that reduce their anxiety, make them more aware and help them engage in those key processes that mastering the student role requires.

The *assessor* focuses on the appraisal of the basic academic skills and competencies of students. The assessor wants to understand whether students can master the skill base of the student role, and whether there are issues or needs that students must address in order to get ready for involvement in higher or post-secondary education. The assessor may not take students through the process of identifying their academic strengths or limitations, but in many cases will co-ordinate the testing and diagnostic resources of the institution to make sure that students have opportunities to appraise their strengths and needs.

Any readiness development programme will probably bring together the four roles of counsellor, interpreter and information provider, guide, and assessor and their distinctive activities into one framework. This is because the fostering of student readiness requires clarification of direction, commitment and expectations (counselling), basic information about requirements (information provision), experience in how to make the institution work for the student (guidance) and basic information about academic skills (assessment). All of these help students to prepare themselves for their engagement with a new world, a world that they may not quite understand because they have not been exposed to it through direct experience, family role models or their secondary educational experience. Facilitation of readiness may integrate these roles into one helper who can bring together for a student or a small group of students counselling, information provision, guidance and assessment. Or the retention programme may integrate these roles into a team structure that is composed of functional specialists, each with a specific role and set of activities. However they are organized, the facilitation of readiness does require helping each student to prepare successfully for the new world of campus life.

ROLES RELEVANT TO THE FACILITATION OF SUPPORT

The facilitation of support benefits from a foundation of readiness. Students who are ready to engage in the role of student may soon discover that they lack key resources to be successful. Students who thought that they were ready, or who felt that they did not need counselling, information, guidance or assessment may soon find that they do indeed need basic assistance that helps them to further their readiness for involvement in higher or post-secondary education. Other students will plunge ahead and discover that they can benefit from augmented support when they face challenges or issues they did not anticipate. The facilitation of support may become important in the lives of many students and a retention programme may find that its principal business lies in helping students to organize these supports. As we described in Chapter 1, these supports may come in the form of emotional support and sustenance, informational support, instrumental support, material support and identity support. These supports help students to persist, perhaps in the face of great challenges, and to continue their education by reducing the stress in their lives.

The role of *resource developer* can help students to organize all these supports. The resource developer may, for example, help students organize self-help groups among commuting students or among students with particular learning needs (identity support). Among the most important resources that a facilitator can put in place are those that help students to come together to share their experiences as students (emotional support), to help one another identify opportunities (informational support) and to help one another get the know-how to navigate college systems like financial advice (instrumental support). In addition, the resource developer may help students to get the material assistance they require to address their housing, transport, income and health care needs (material support). In this area, the resource developer is conscious of what students need in order to be successful and may create new partnerships both inside and outside the institution to create new resources. For example, the resource developer can help set up student houses that enable students to live off-campus in an affordable manner with other students, thereby preventing isolation.

The *skill developer* may focus on the acquisition by students of the 'nuts and bolts' skills they need to achieve success academically, socially and personally. The skill developer in a retention programme may create skill-building opportunities and educational options for students as they move through different phases in their careers in higher education. Students learn about the options available to them and the career and vocational implications of their choices. The skill developer may create an informal curriculum to help students learn about how to apply for various post-graduate opportunities or how to position themselves for scholarships or fellowships. In one institution, the retention programme offers instruction on the development of skills in how to build relationships with teaching staff, interact with staff in the classroom, secure assistance from staff, and build a mentoring relationship with staff. The skill developer in this case is herself a member of the teaching staff who prides herself in helping first-year students, particularly older women returning to education after a period of absence, to 'learn the ropes' of higher education.

The facilitation of support may also come about through the *mentor* role. Here students have opportunities to be matched with someone who will build a personalized and strong relationship with them. The mentor identifies with the situation of the student and is willing to form a common bond that encompasses caring, the teaching of skills (instrumental support), the fostering of identity, assistance with the resolution of problems and help in networking with other people, groups or institutions that can offer opportunities to the student.

Mentoring can establish a close and warm working relationship between the student and the mentor. It is an informal role that is formally sanctioned only in that the retention programme helps mentors and students to establish their relationships. It may be a very powerful role in that it enables the student to have access to someone who will be flexible, responsive and accessible. It is powerful in that the mentor may be able to open up some doors that would otherwise be closed to the student. For example, the mentor can help a student find summer employment, obtain a paid traineeship or qualify for an award sponsored by a professional association. Perhaps the measure of the effectiveness of a mentor is found in the doors it opens for students, and the opportunities that mentors can help students find. In a successful case, the student will identify with the mentor, who will become an important role model in relationship to the student's choices about education, career and personal conduct.

The facilitation of support helps students to persist. They can get the resources they need to keep going as students and to secure the skills they need to execute the role of student successfully. Mentoring as the facilitation of support combines numerous supports informally into one role. Mentoring can personalize the educational experience for students while it can open up opportunities that might otherwise remain closed to them. Good mentoring makes students feel special, accepted and valued. It can offer them the hope and vision they need to persist in their education.

ROLES RELEVANT TO OVERCOMING OR DEFEATING BARRIERS

Many students will face serious obstacles to educational achievement. Some will be overwhelmed by personal stress triggered by changes in their family, financial position or health. Others will face academic challenges that reveal learning needs or issues, while yet others will face abuse, harassment or even violence during the course of their education. Even the best students may experience periods in which barriers emerge that seem impossible to overcome or navigate alone. They may not know where to turn, or they may experience shame or guilt and as a consequence be reluctant to seek help from anyone.

A good retention programme offers roles that help students to address such barriers, and may offer intensive services during particular periods of the academic careers of students that may then taper off as the students become more able to pursue their education without such support. Some of these services may be integrated into the retention programme itself while others may operate in other programme areas that sustain a connection with the retention programme, such as in student advice services, victim assistance, mental health services or health care services. The retention programme that is well integrated into the institution will create these linkages and will help other student service providers to understand the retention implications of how they work with students. For example, a victim assistance programme may offer an immediate referral of a student to retention services so that the student can make arrangements for a non-punitive academic leave, short-term relief from academic demands and assistance with staying abreast of education while addressing other needs. Well-thought-out linkages that form a 'retention network' may enable any student service programme to trigger those retention services that can facilitate the student's continued involvement in his or her education.

The retention programme will want to become sensitive to the barriers individual students face and, since many of these arise with some urgency, the role of *crisis intervenor and troubleshooter* is relevant to any retention effort. We define a crisis as any unexpected event that creates considerable stress in a student, who perceives the event as serious, and that results in diminished functioning for a period of time. Diminished functioning can express itself in the student withdrawing from his or her educational activities and responsibilities and in a diminished ability to handle academic expectations such that the student's status is in jeopardy. Students in crisis probably manifest a marked change in their educational performance, moving quickly from effective or good performance to poor performance. Teaching staff notice this change in performance, while fellow students see directly the toll of the crisis. A student in crisis may become withdrawn, depressed, irritable or even hostile, and may demonstrate a marked change in mood and in sleeping, eating and thinking.

The crisis intervention role within the retention programme strengthens the ability of the programme to reach out and work with students who find themselves in crisis. Students may make contact with the retention programme on their own initiative because of a prior relationship with facilitators. These students may present themselves in considerable emotional distress and they will probably be preoccupied by their academic concerns and needs yet feel unable to address them. Crises are often academic in nature and they are simple to identify, such as stress created during examinations or when students feel overwhelmed by work and academic expectations. In these cases, the crisis intervenor will help students to identify the academic situation, reduce their distress, restore cognitive appraisal and problem-solving processes and formulate a plan to address the academic issue they face. In serious academic situations it may take about three sessions for students to overcome their crisis, during which the crisis intervenor within the retention programme sticks with the student, scheduling the meetings close together in time so that a resolution is achieved in a timely manner. As a troubleshooter, the member of staff may need to address discrete issues as part of a short-term plan, for example contacting and meeting key teaching staff to bring about a temporary reduction in academic expectations or helping the student to make short-term financial arrangements.

What is important here is that the crisis intervenor works with the student to identify and execute a plan to resolve the crisis with an outcome of minimizing the impact on the student's persistence or preventing the student from dropping out of education. The plan divides the responsibility between the intervenor and the student. The intervenor is practical and task-oriented, giving the student only the responsibilities he or she can handle at the time, fully cognizant that the student's functioning is compromised and avoiding further overloading the student with additional responsibilities he or she cannot readily handle.

There will be other cases when student crises are precipitated by life events other than academic ones alone, but which will still result in serious limitations in the ability to function academically. Serious life events may require the retention programme to steer students to other helping resources, yet staff members of the retention programme can remain involved with these students. Crisis intervention and troubleshooting in this context may mean that the retention programme helps students to generate a plan to support their academic retention and persistence while other care providers address the serious problems that students present and must resolve. The retention programme staff member who offers crisis intervention may find that he or she is working as a member of a team that assists students to bring together the resources to resolve the crisis and to restore their functioning. As a team member, the retention programme staff member targets the troubleshooting of academic issues that must be addressed to sustain students and foster persistence.

There is one more role worth noting in this area. The *advocate* is particularly important in helping students to navigate situations in which they experience discrimination, oppression, abuse and harassment. In these situations, students need someone who is dedicated to them. The advocate hears students out, helps them to understand their situation and helps them to formulate a plan to address their situation. The advocate then assists them to implement the plan in order to bring about a desired outcome.

The advocacy role: an example

One student, for example, has a serious disability, and the technical college she attends will not help her to make an appropriate accommodation to address her learning needs. Indeed, the administrators of the school are hostile towards her requests and discount the legitimacy of the disability even though she offers corroborating medical evidence to support her claim. The student becomes so agitated that she is soon labelled as a problem among other students and staff. She decides to withdraw from college, thinking that she cannot deal with what she refers to as 'bureaucratic red tape'. However, she discovers that someone in the college will serve in an advocacy role and help her navigate the bureaucracy so that she can make a claim and have a hearing.

The advocate is devoted to the student and to helping her realize the outcome of an appropriate accommodation. The advocate helps her to develop and carry out a plan. Like a mentor, the advocate forms a strong relationship with the student and offers her emotional support and instrumental assistance in terms of guidance on how to handle her request. The advocate links her to other students with disabilities, and maintains close contact as the student begins to implement the plan. The advocate continues to offer information about whom to contact and assists the student in gaining the skills she needs to make her claim. The advocate suggests to the student that she will be reluctant to act directly on behalf of the student but will back her up when she needs assistance, yet the advocate also suggests that she will step in and offer representation if the student requests it but only if the student feels that she can no longer represent herself.

The advocate need not come from within the university but may come from an external source such as a rights protection and advocacy organization. It is important to underscore that the advocate still serves in a retention role. She facilitates the student's persistence in the face of a bureaucracy that the student says is failing to work for her. The advocate role is an example of how a retention programme with an external sponsorship can enter the picture when there is considerable conflict. The advocate does not represent the institution and does not try to mediate between the institution and the student. The advocate represents the student. It is probably a retention role that is best used in those situations in which there is considerable conflict, where there appears to be no other option for the student.

CONCLUSION AND GUIDELINES

We do not offer a rigid role framework within this chapter, but recommend a very flexible approach to the retention roles that staff members can make use of in fostering the retention of students. We link the roles to what we consider to be the three most important functions. These are developing readiness, mustering support, and overcoming or defeating barriers. Those who facilitate retention should think about the function they are trying to achieve with and on behalf of students and then begin to match the helping role to this function.

For example, when helping students develop their readiness, a facilitator may become a guide who helps them to understand the institution and the resources it offers to them as individuals who are getting used to participating in higher or post-secondary education. The facilitator may integrate the role of guide with that of interpreter. As a student executes various 'assignments' designed to help him or her to become comfortable in the institution and familiar with its resources, the facilitator interprets what the student is learning and steers that student to additional information, perhaps about various courses, services and opportunities.

Although there are distinctions among the roles, retention programme staff are facilitators first, with a number of different roles available to them for the achievement of the various functions that bring about the outcome of student persistence and retention. Thus, the roles become tools in the realization of outcomes that pertain to role mastery, academic success, persistence and, ultimately, retention.

11

Dimension 5: The helping process in retention

MAIN POINTS OF THE CHAPTER

- Forming strong relationships with students is the bedrock of the helping process in retention.
- The helping process in retention requires the linkage of students' reasons for being in higher education to their aspirations. This gives meaning to students and helps them to understand their educational purpose.
- Helping students to identify their needs, the barriers they face and the supports they require can result in the formulation of the retention plan.
- The retention plan brings together those supports, services and activities that taken together assist students to persist in their education.
- Troubleshooting and preventing issues from disrupting the academic life of students are essential to proactive retention.
- The retention helping process is dynamic and should change as students change their circumstances, aspirations and academic direction.
- Once the plan is successfully executed the helping process links students to the next set of experiences or opportunities.
- Re-entry into the helping process once it is complete should be easy for students. They should be able easily to trigger the use of the programme when they confront issues that threaten their success and persistence.

Student retention and persistence is a major outcome of a systematic process of helping students to move forward in their academic careers. This systematic process follows many of the principles and ideas identified in earlier chapters. We can simplify this process through the consolidation of a handful of practices that teaching staff, student development staff and others can use to facilitate student retention and persistence. These practices taken together form the helping process in retention.

Those familiar with the provision of human services will find that this process reflects the practices and processes that counsellors, social workers and others use to help people. Other people, whose expertise does not reside in human services, may not be familiar with this process but nonetheless they may have an intuitive or tacit sense of how to undertake the helping process in retention. In their academic roles, they may help students to achieve academic and career aims, and they may interact with students through crisis intervention, counselling and mentoring roles, as noted in the previous chapter.

THE RETENTION HELPING PROCESS IN A NUTSHELL

In a nutshell, the helping process in retention involves the following set of seven practices:

1. There are initial contacts with students that offer the retention facilitator an opportunity to form a relationship with them, get to know their aspirations and understand their educational and personal backgrounds.
2. The retention facilitator engages students in a process of relating their aspirations to a retention aim or goal, and conducts an informal assessment of the barriers or issues students face in achieving this aim or goal.
3. The retention facilitator and students collaborate in the identification of relevant supports that are useful to achieving the retention aim or goal.
4. The retention facilitator and students develop individual retention and persistence plans. A retention and persistence plan brings together the aspirations, retention aim, barrier identification and development of supports into an overall strategy for achieving specific outcomes that help students to be successful in their academic careers.
5. The facilitator and students implement these plans by fostering an ongoing student support system and by troubleshooting retention and persistence issues in an anticipatory manner or as they emerge.
6. The facilitator engages students in an ongoing monitoring and evaluation of their plans. They make modifications according to the changing situation of students, changes in their aspirations or changes in the academic direction they take.
7. When students achieve the substance of the plan, the facilitator helps them to put closure on their experience, conduct a summative evaluation of the plan and link them to the next set of experiences or activities in their academic careers.

We do not want to be overly prescriptive about this process since it is up to each institution of post-secondary or higher education to develop a retention helping process that makes sense to its culture, staff and, most of all, students, but offer a skeletal outline of the process so as to show student retention facilitators a basic logic for structuring it.

There are three important aspects of the process we propose. First, a critical product of the helping process is the formulation of a plan that is useful to the student. Second, and perhaps most important, the plan forms a collaboration between the student and the facilitator that is implemented by these two individuals working together. And third, the implementation of the plan increases the chances that the student stays in higher or post-secondary education by fulfilling the role that the institution and the student's aspirations require of him or her. Thus, the retention and persistence plan should guide a student in mastering those aspects of the student role that are necessary to staying in post-secondary or higher education successfully.

These practices should not be undertaken in a rigid or formalistic manner. We hope that each student who has retention and persistence needs will experience this process in an informal yet potent manner. The retention plan is probably committed to writing, but it is an informal document that students can modify at any time as their lives and their minds change. Retention and persistence plans should 'follow the student' and change as the student changes as a result of participation in post-secondary or higher education.

PRACTICE I: INITIAL STUDENT CONTACT

As we noted in Chapter 9, an effective outreach process will bring students into a retention programme looking for assistance. They may come to the programme anxious and confused. Someone may have told them that they are not performing well or that they do not appear to be either excited about involvement in higher education or committed to the educational process as the institution defines it. Concern from an academic counsellor may result in a follow-up contact with a student to offer him or her the opportunity to participate in a retention programme or activity. A committed member of the teaching staff may reach out to students at a crucial time of the term to identify those who are not doing well academically and then steer them in the direction of a retention programme. A psychotherapist may link a student to the programme after that student has come to the institution's mental health facility in crisis. A family crisis or economic situation may be disrupting the student's educational progress, and the psychotherapist may want the student to have added support even though this is for a limited time period.

There are many routes to the retention programme. Indeed, an effective programme that is well integrated into college life offers a number of different portals through which students can learn about retention opportunities. There are a number of gatekeepers dispersed throughout the institution who can direct, steer or link students to such a resource.

But nonetheless students will present themselves at the initial contact in different ways. Some students will be in denial. They may be hostile, and angry with the members of staff, counsellor or other gatekeeper who steered them to the retention programme. Other students will be in a state of confusion, particularly if they are in some sort of crisis, personal, family or other, that places them in a state of disequilibrium. Some students will be passive since they are convinced that they cannot master what the educational institution requires of them. Still others may be highly motivated but without a full understanding of how they should proceed to avert a potentially negative outcome like educational failure and subsequent withdrawal.

There is probably an array of conditions that students will present. The initial contact with students coming for retention assistance offers facilitators opportunities to get students focused on the issues they face in mastering the student role, and to help them identify initially their retention needs. The most important outcome of the initial contact lies in relationship formation. The initial contact offers facilitators opportunities to express a personal interest in students and their situations. Warmth and caring signal to students that the apparently impersonal, high-performance environment of the university has a human face to it. The facilitator communicates to students seeking retention assistance that he or she cares as a person and as an institutional representative.

The retention relationship is fortified when students experience facilitators who listen, gently inquire and explore students' understanding of what brings them to the retention programme. In this engagement, students have an opportunity to identify the manner in which they were steered to the programme, why they were told to make this contact and what triggered the linkage. The facilitator wants the students' interpretation of events, not to judge but to help students clarify their own desire to engage in an effort of retention.

Clarification of these events allows facilitators to identify how the retention and persistence programme operates. It allows facilitators to describe what services the programme offers and how it can be put to use by students in their efforts to master their situation and begin to defeat the issues that may be jeopardizing their continued persistence in post-secondary or higher education. With this knowledge about why they have come to the retention programme and what the programme can offer them, students can make decisions about whether they want to participate in the services, opportunities and activities the programme offers. Helping students to make such decisions reinforces their commitment, motivation and responsibility. It is an early message in the process, and indicates that retention is a collaborative process beginning with a student's decision to move ahead.

The initial contact can continue to help students and facilitators to groom their working relationships. Students who are clear about why they have come to the programme, and who feel a sense of responsibility for their involvement, are getting ready to move forward to create a new situation that facilitates their success. Retention facilitators make use of this emerging commitment in a tactical way. They engage students in a dialogue about what brought them to post-secondary or higher education, why they want to remain and what they aspire to as a result of their education. Students will vary in their responses and in their clarity. Some will have limited academic self-concepts while others will have strong ones. Whatever facilitators discover should not allow them to 'write off' students but should add to their growing understanding of their students and the issues those students must address to master the role of student.

This information base grows as facilitators inquire into the educational and personal backgrounds of their students. They will learn much about the students' attitudes towards education, and how these were formed. Knowledge of previous academic experiences, performances and skills will help the astute facilitator gain a better understanding of the academic challenges students currently face. And the identification and elaboration of the personal backgrounds of students may offer even more insight into the challenges they face.

The helping process: an example

Sally's experience can help us to understand the initial contact better. She is referred to the retention programme of the school of nursing because she failed in two core courses. The two members of staff who teach these courses tell Sally that she needs to consult the retention facilitator of the school because her present performance will lead to her dismissal from the undergraduate nursing programme. Sally feels that she is doing everything possible to master the two courses, and she thinks that the two members of staff are harsh, inconsiderate and uncaring. Yet the members of staff are telling her in no uncertain terms that her place on the course is in jeopardy, something she knows but will not admit.

The retention facilitator quickly schedules a meeting with Sally, who arrives at the appointment late and very sullen and hostile. The facilitator inquires into what brought Sally to the retention programme, which stimulates a considerable amount of anger from Sally. The facilitator listens to her, and asks her about her perceptions of the actions of the members of staff and the content of the courses.

The facilitator moves through this material attentively but quickly, and focuses on why Sally wants to enter the nursing profession. Here, Sally's demeanour changes and she becomes quite positive as she relates the personal experiences that brought her to professional education in nursing. The facilitator as a prac-tising nurse relates to what Sally shares with her and they begin to discuss the entire curriculum and the challenges it presents to new students. The relationship changes in a positive way the more they speak and share. The facilitator then describes the retention programme and how it can serve Sally to resolve difficulties, both at this time and later. Sally voices surprise that she even has a future on the course, something the facilitator reinforces as both possible and probable if they can get over the current issues.

The facilitator believes that Sally is now in a position to address the issues openly in some depth. It is not surprising to find that there are a number of academic and personal issues that interact to create a great deal of stress in Sally's life. One issue is that she works almost full time, and finds it difficult to integrate the roles of worker and student, particularly in a highly demanding course like nursing. She does not have the time to invest in the two courses, both of which require a considerable amount of new learning on her part. She has very high expectations for herself both in her work and in her schooling and she is failing to do either well. She has not found any additional sources of financial support as an alternative to full-time employment. The facilitator suggests that they continue their work together, and Sally agrees, as she finds the facilitator sympathetic.

PRACTICE II: FORMULATING A RETENTION AIM

So, why are students involved in post-secondary or higher education? What are their aspirations and how stable are these in relationship to the career or vocational direction students wish to pursue? These are important issues that are within the scope of the retention programme as outlined in Chapter 7. Aspirations are important because they give students a reason for staying in post-secondary or higher education. They can serve as reference points for students as they become frustrated with the process of delaying gratification in preparation for the next steps in their lives.

Helping students to reflect on their aspirations is no easy step. Students may find it frustrating, as may their retention facilitators. Although a full process of career counselling or development is probably not appropriate at this stage, nonetheless it is an important step in the process of student retention to identify the academic purpose of students and why academic work makes sense to them. It is not unusual for students to vary in their maturity here. Some students may be able to articulate their academic purpose, while others may be tentative or confused. Aspirations sometimes derive from parents and families, who may hold them more strongly than students do. Some students may be pursuing one academic path while they have preferences for another academic path they have not shared with anyone. Exploring these preferences, ideas or self-conceptions may form the very anchor the retention process needs to secure the persistence of students. A retention helping process that assists students to revisit these aspirations, form them or evaluate them may be fundamental to the achievement of student persistence.

The clarification of aspirations may help students to come to grips with the need to achieve success in certain periods of their education when their academic requirements do not make full sense to them. Students who have difficulty with the required courses of a core curriculum may feel that they do not have the motivation to invest in these courses since they do not like them or do not feel skilled in them. The retention programme may need to demonstrate to students how an introductory knowledge of basic subjects can be meaningful and useful to them in achieving their career, vocational or personal aspirations. Coming to grips with the student role and what it requires may help students to enhance their academic self-concepts, feelings of mastery and ability to engage in self-directed education.

The clarification of aspirations (or their absence) can help frame the retention aim or goal. There are two key questions here for students to answer, depending on how they frame their education. What do they want to achieve that will increase their persistence? What do they need to achieve to increase their persistence? Most students will have to achieve a balance between 'want' and 'need' by finding personal purpose and meaning and by engaging in behaviour that will improve their chances of succeeding academically. For example, the student and facilitator may frame the retention aim as follows: 'David will successfully complete the core curriculum of the college so that he can progress to the vocational arts course that he wants to pursue. A retention aim need not be so expansive but may be focused, like the following: 'David will complete foundation courses in algebra, composition and computer literacy before his formal enrolment into college.'

Of course, the ultimate aim of retention is to help students to persist to the end of a course of study. The selection of a retention aim focuses the attention of the student and the facilitator on an outcome that will improve the students' chances of being successful. The student and facilitator identify an overarching aim that will serve as the focus of the individual student retention and persistence plan. The student and facilitator should focus on one aim at a time that:

- makes sense to the student;
- is relevant to student retention and persistence;
- will help the student to remain enrolled and achieving satisfactory results.

Identification, framing and formulation of this retention aim or goal require considerable dialogue between the student and the facilitator. Often institutions enrol students in group-oriented retention programmes where they receive exposure to the culture of the institution, opportunities to develop academic skills, and career clarification. These programmes are invaluable but they may force students into learning situations that do not substantively address the students' own retention issues as they experience them and as they frame them. Fortunately, many of these kinds of programmes help students to forge a personal relationship with a mentor who can help them to identify a retention aim and then make a plan to achieve it.

The nursing retention facilitator is one such resource to Sally. The instructors of the two courses in which Sally was not performing well could have referred her to an extra course or tutoring. However, teaching staff understand that all students present their own academic issues. Students with deficits or challenges that are primarily academic will need opportunities for tutorial or developmental work. Students with personal issues that interact with academic ones may need opportunities for enhanced counselling and guidance. The school understands that all students need an opportunity to sort out their own retention aims before they are steered in a specific direction or prescribed a specific course.

Sally and the retention facilitator must address two realities. First, Sally has to work at least part time, and second, she must achieve adequate academic performance in two courses, the content of which requires new learning on her part. Sally has high expectations of herself both as a worker and as a student, which means that, although this aim may sound straightforward, she needs to examine and change her expectations or increase her performance if she is to be successful in higher education. This is not an easy task. The aim Sally and the retention facilitator identify is as follows:

Sally will complete all core courses with acceptable academic performance while still working part time, and will get the assistance she needs to achieve this kind of performance. She will relax her expectations of herself as a worker, and will maintain high academic standards while she pursues the help she needs to be successful in the core curriculum of nursing education.

There is perhaps another aspect to Sally's aim. Her income is important to her family. Members of Sally's social network may also need to change their expectations about Sally as a student and worker. This may require considerable family work that may be out of the scope of the facilitation of retention. The retention facilitator, however, may want to steer Sally in a direction that will help her to address these issues, and to resolve them in a manner that helps her to continue as a nursing student.

The facilitation of retention in this aspect of the helping process requires the identification and appraisal of so-called barriers. It is important for retention facilitators to refrain from setting up expectations of students that their situations or environments can defeat. The identification of barriers may sound too negative, but barriers can threaten the achievement of a retention aim if the student and facilitator ignore them, fail to identify them or fail to resolve them. The retention facilitator does not question Sally's commitment to becoming a member of the nursing profession, but she does understand that Sally performs in a very dense network of expectations that she, her teachers and her family perpetuate. The student and facilitator must appraise these expectations and identify how they can change without relaxing academic expectations. Failure to engage in this process of barrier identification and appraisal may result in the defeat of Sally's aim. A good plan must incorporate a keen sense for what barriers to address.

PRACTICE III: IDENTIFICATION OF RELEVANT SUPPORTS

In the conclusion to Chapter 1 we defined what we mean by 'support for retention'. It is here that we underscore the importance of support as it pertains to helping students to master the role of student. The 'role of student' may be defined in different ways by different institutions but, however it is defined, adequate and appropriate support is essential to effective role performance. It requires the matching of resources to student needs. As a result students are more likely to master the role of student and perform in a manner that brings them academic success as they and/or the educational institution defines it. As we noted previously, the astute retention facilitator will help students to integrate what they want in terms of academic success with what the institution wants in terms of success. This does not mean that the student merely surrenders to institutional demands. Perhaps the best practice of retention involves helping students to discover how they can meet their own aspirations by making the educational institution work for them.

In Chapter 1, we identified five forms of retention support: emotional sustenance, informational support, instrumental support, material support and identity support. The mustering and matching of supports are the tools of the retention effort. They enable the retention facilitator to link substantive helping resources to the performance, tasks and activities students must engage in within the context of their course of study. *Emotional sustenance*, for example, may be a very critical support to students who tend to get isolated, and who may attribute their lack of academic, career or personal success to themselves alone. Despite their academic gifts and talents, students who lack emotional sustenance may be in jeopardy in terms of persistence. They may have little information about how an institution operates, what staff to select and how to make use of the 'system' to their own advantage. Without a peer network, and without guidance from more informed students, they may discontinue their work when they confront an impasse. Likewise, students in crisis may feel as though they have no one to whom to turn for assistance. They may find their cognitive abilities diminished during challenging academic times or when relationship or interpersonal problems come to the foreground.

The retention helping process needs to incorporate emotional sustenance. Those who staff the retention programme should have training in interpersonal skills in order to engage students effectively, particularly at times when students may require (and benefit from) emotional support the most.

Group approaches to helping may be important vehicles for offering emotional support to students. Students who learn to support one another, and to offer empathic and sympathetic responses will probably reduce their feelings of isolation, and will realize that they are not the only ones who need or desire retention assistance. Groups that offer self-help and mutual support may be an effective and efficient way to offer emotional assistance to students who become involved in retention programmes. Even if groups cannot convene physically, they may perpetuate emotional sustenance through e-mail, chat rooms and online dialogues.

For example, Sally may benefit from membership in a group composed of nursing students who are juggling work and family responsibilities. The retention facilitator helps to convene the group, acquire the resources to keep it going and integrate it into the life of the school. The group is responsible for helping new members to join and for keeping meetings going. Group meetings help Sally to understand the stresses she experiences, and to talk about these first-hand with other students experiencing the same kind of concerns. Sally finds out that she is not alone and that her feelings are not unique but fairly consistent with the emotional reactions of her peers.

Informational support is an important support for students who need to obtain more information about the student role and about institutional requirements and resources. Timely and useful academic information may help students to understand academic expectations. It may also help them to appreciate the choices they can make about courses, staff and curricula. Sally, for example, might decide to drop her two core courses after speaking with some fellow students who suggest taking them over the summer from different members of teaching staff who are a better match to her learning style. Although this does not relieve her of the responsibility for mastering the content of the courses, it does give her a sense of more control over how and when she takes these courses. Sally wonders why her academic tutor did not suggest the same option. She realizes that there is a diversity of information that is highly influenced by perspective and role. One of the conclusions she arrives at is that she needs relationships with more experienced students who can help her to access information that works for her. The nursing retention facilitator puts her in contact with the school's student organization, which will help her to access such relationships and a diversity of student-driven information about the curriculum.

Instrumental support focuses on the task at hand. How will students complete required courses? How will they develop the skills they need to progress through the curriculum? How will they obtain skills they should have obtained during an earlier period of education? Sally, for example, needs substantive help. Fortunately, there are instrumental supports that will help her to master the new learning material that she requires. Available to the retention facilitator are several advanced undergraduate and post-graduate students who serve as tutors in the core curriculum. These students are comfortable with the material Sally must master, they are good teachers and they are flexible to accommodate Sally's schedule. As well as instructing Sally in her courses, they can offer emotional sustenance and information. With this extra assistance, Sally feels she can master the learning challenge she faces. Indeed, good instrumental assistance should help people feel that they can meet a challenge, and resolve it in a successful manner. In relationship to retention, instrumental assistance means helping a student to identify a problem and obtain the technical assistance to resolve it. Often problems pertain to academic preparation and course completion, or to study skills, personal organization, or planning and maintaining a timetable.

The importance of *material support* emerges when students have basic resource challenges or issues that can disrupt their educational performance and persistence. The doctoral student who holds down two part-time jobs, teaches part time and pursues her own studies may be in jeopardy of burning out or ill health. A member of staff who helps the student to secure a fellowship may help her to make ends meet and focus on the completion of course work or dissertation. Without it the student's material situation may be inadequate to support involvement in full-time doctoral studies.

Material support may involve assistance with housing, transport, clothing, books, nutrition, childcare and tuition. Creating material supports may be a fundamental strategy for facilitating access to higher education among students in poverty or close to poverty because they must postpone involvement in gainful employment.

This kind of support is important to Sally. Both Sally and the nursing retention facilitator understand that she must reduce her involvement in work and prioritize her nursing education. Helping Sally to obtain material support or financial aid is an important feature of her retention plan.

Identity support becomes an important feature of retention for those students who need to define themselves and make sense of who they are in order to persist in their educational careers. Identity as a support for retention may help students to fashion a strong understanding of why they want to pursue higher education. For Sally, her identity as a working family member who can carry her own weight is a critical aspect of her retention. She has to balance work and student roles, but perhaps not to the extent of doing both full time. Her involvement in a group of 'working nursing students' that offers emotional support and respects her identity may help sustain her efforts over the course of her undergraduate career.

Putting supports into place for all students involved in retention helps to stop or slow down the problems or issues that may be leading them to a decision about ending their involvement in higher education. Putting supports in place will help students to meet role and life challenges that involvement in higher education creates and will also help students to reduce barriers that can otherwise disrupt their involvement. Matching supports to student needs is the essence of a student-centred approach to retention. It is important to involve students directly in the identification of the supports that they feel will meet their needs. Thus, retention facilitators should engage students in a dialogue about what emotional, informational, instrumental, material and identity supports they feel they need to address the barriers or challenges they face. This is what personalizes retention for each student.

PRACTICE IV: THE INDIVIDUAL STUDENT RETENTION PLAN

The retention plan is 'individualized' in that it refers directly to what the student seeks to achieve and what help or assistance he or she needs or wants in order to achieve the desired retention aim. The individual student retention plan enables the student and the facilitator to bring together the work of the previous steps of the retention helping process into a focused and organized perspective about what work will be undertaken to keep the student in higher education. By the time the student and facilitator initiate the plan, they possess a great deal of relevant information that they can organize into it:

- The student's aspirations are known, and the student and facilitator understand their potency and their clarity.
- There is an understanding of the student's educational and personal background and how these influence retention and persistence.
- A retention aim or goal is identified and agreed upon by the student and facilitator.
- The barriers the student faces are identified and there is a provisional sense of how to address them.
- The supports the student needs to achieve the retention aim or goal are identified.

These are the key ingredients of the individual student retention plan. The plan does not have to be formal although it is important to commit it to writing. To underscore the student's and facilitator's commitment to executing their responsibilities, each party signs the plan to acknowledge these responsibilities. Each party will probably have specific tasks to carry out in order to achieve the spirit and substance of the plan. The plan will serve as a way to give direction to each party as they work separately and together to achieve the retention aim. The plan also lends itself to evaluation in order to determine if it is working, whether it needs to be revised or whether the retention aim has been achieved and the student is ready to move on.

Sally's plan incorporates her aspirations to join the nursing profession, and identifies the retention aim of helping her to make progress toward this. The plan identifies the barriers Sally experiences in the achievement of retention and persistence, and it presents the supports that Sally and the facilitator will bring together in order to achieve the aim. The plan identifies Sally's role in the achievement of each support as well as the role of the facilitator. One support is that Sally and the facilitator will maintain their working relationship during the course of the retention plan. The plan also incorporates the specific outcomes Sally seeks to achieve. A time frame is established within the plan to guide the evaluation of progress at milestone intervals, and to conduct an overall evaluation of the merits of the plan.

Placing the information the retention helping process captures into a written document helps students and facilitators to gain a sense of direction and offers them something to monitor and evaluate. A written plan can also provide a boost to students' morale and motivation when they see that they can turn their situation around and obtain support in doing so. The plan communicates to students that they have a substantive set of aspirations. It communicates that they are enrolled in post-secondary or higher education for good reasons, and that the fulfilment of their aims will help them to surmount their difficulties.

A retention plan that is truly individualized and student-centred is a powerful tool to incorporate into the retention helping process. It enables students and facilitators to move into the action that the achievement of retention requires.

PRACTICE V: IMPLEMENTATION OF THE RETENTION PLAN

The retention plan offers guidance to students and facilitators in the achievement of the retention aim. It is also a guide to implementation since a good plan identifies the responsibilities and representative roles of facilitator and student. A student, for example, may be responsible for attending a peer support group after a facilitator has assisted him or her to identify a relevant resource. A facilitator may be responsible for organizing the testing that students require so they can identify their learning styles and learning needs.

The formulation of the retention plan may be quite simple compared to its actual implementation. Students and facilitators will find that its implementation is quite a challenge as they persist in the face of busy schedules and competing demands and priorities. However, implementation of the retention plan is 'retention in action' since it requires facilitators and students to be vigilant about what they need to achieve, and responsible in following through on the arrangement and completion of necessary activities. Consistent implementation becomes one of the primary ingredients of success.

A consistent meeting schedule between facilitator and student may be essential to effective implementation. Meetings do not have to be long, but they need to be frequent enough to give the implementation of the retention plan a serious character and to underscore its importance to the achievement of the retention aim. The focus of these frequent meetings is fourfold. First, it enables the facilitator and the student to continue to strengthen and build their working relationship as it pertains to retention. Second, frequent meetings allow the facilitator and the student to review the retention plan, become familiar with its content and anticipate the activities that need to be implemented and completed in order to bring the plan into reality. Third, frequent meetings allow the plan to be updated or modified. The retention plan is not cast in stone and there should be ample opportunity for the facilitator and student to identify ways that the plan can be improved and to identify the addition, modification or deletion of retention activities and tasks. And fourth, frequent meetings allow timely crisis or urgent intervention. Students who come to sessions consistently may bring timely issues that, if not addressed immediately, compromise retention and persistence. If the retention work is sufficiently proactive, these crises will probably fall by the wayside over a short period of time, and the work of student development can take place in the spheres of academic, personal and career development.

The meetings that take place between facilitator and student can be structured enough to give them a 'business' tone. Facilitators and students examine retention plans closely enough to be able to formulate relevant agendas that guide the substance and process of these meetings. For example, Sally and her retention facilitator formulate a meeting agenda with the following elements:

1. friendly visiting;
2. identification and discussion of immediate or pressing issues;
3. evaluation of Sally's current retention status and overall progress in terms of retention outcomes;
4. review of current activities and tasks and the status of these;
5. identification and resolution of barriers to the completion of activities and tasks;
6. review of the retention plan and the identification of additional activities and tasks;
7. establishment of the next outcome and Sally's and the facilitator's responsibilities for the achievement of the outcome;
8. closure and schedule of the next meeting.

Sally and her facilitator stick closely to this agenda since it works for them, helps them to focus their energies and keeps them mindful of the retention plan, that is, its aim, important outcomes, and relevant activities and tasks. Although they use this agenda as their framework for meetings, they find that over time their meetings become less frequent. The retention helping process they have undertaken follows three phases.

The retention helping process may be characterized first by an urgent, initial phase in which Sally feels compelled to reach out to the facilitator since her place on the course is threatened. Sally and the facilitator meet at least once a week, and they are in more frequent contact by voice and electronic mail. Sally feels very dependent on the facilitator during this phase, and the facilitator feels the intensity of this dependency.

With consistent work on the retention plan, this phase yields to a middle phase in which Sally's dependency decreases and the work becomes less urgent. A calm sets in and Sally feels confident that with the support of the facilitator she can master the retention challenges she faces. Although meetings are still consistent, they begin to decrease in frequency. Sally and the facilitator might meet only a couple of times a month but they make considerable progress on retention outcomes.

The ending phase emerges when Sally begins to consolidate her learning, and takes more independent or autonomous action. The facilitator during this phase begins to let go, but is still available to troubleshoot Sally's concerns and issues. Even in this phase, Sally may contact the facilitator reporting a crisis but the urgent nature of these contacts has declined. The lessening of the urgent tone suggests that Sally is meeting the challenges of the nursing course successfully with the help of her newly developed support system. As a result, the facilitator now lets go, but remains available for friendly visiting and contact. Sally knows that the facilitator remains an ally, someone she can turn to in the future if there is a need.

The helping process may not be confined to the student–facilitator relationship. The scope of the retention plan in terms of its aim, principal outcomes and task structure may be so broad that it requires the involvement of several different people. The retention plan may foster the creation of a student support team that is composed of people who are dedicated to helping the student to be successful in post-secondary or higher education.

PRACTICE VI: ONGOING MONITORING AND EVALUATION OF THE RETENTION PLAN

It is very important for both students and retention facilitators to understand that these plans are not cast in stone. They can and should be modified as the situations of students improve or worsen, as students master new attitudes, skills and abilities, and as students move on in their academic careers and face new challenges. The 'shelf life' of the retention plan should be the effective dates students and facilitators establish for the work to be done. The facilitator and students implement these plans by fostering an ongoing student support system and by troubleshooting retention and persistence issues in an anticipatory manner or as they emerge.

Embedded in the helping process is an approach to monitoring and evaluation that gives retention a dynamic character. Successful retention means that a student does not merely stay out of crisis, or that crises get resolved in a timely and successful manner. It means that a student's mastery over the role of student increases and that critical psychological outcomes emerge during the helping process like persistence, self-confidence, and clarity about educational, personal, and career goals and options.

The facilitator, student and team engage in an active monitoring and evaluation process. This monitoring process gets actuated in two ways. First, every meeting offers an opportunity to monitor and evaluate the content of the plan in terms of relevance, timeliness and feasibility, the merits of the activities that are undertaken to achieve the plan, and the outcomes that are achieved to make retention a reality. Second, milestone meetings held primarily to evaluate the retention plan help the facilitator, student and team members to focus on whether there is substantial progress being made toward the aim of retention. These milestone meetings lend themselves to steering the overall process, and to ensuring that retention efforts are not only of high quality but also effective in producing the outcomes that the student needs in order to persist in post-secondary or higher education.

By integrating monitoring and evaluation into each meeting, and by holding milestone meetings to conduct a summative evaluation of the retention plan, the retention effort does not become stagnant. The 'shelf life' of the plan is renewed over the duration of the retention helping process, and the student gets a sense of renewal and progress. The student also understands that he or she must become reflective about the experience, since there is the expectation that the plan can and will change. There is the expectation that the student will reflect on what is needed to make retention happen, and that the student will feel free to report these needs as they come up in his or her lived experience.

Monitoring and evaluation do not have to be the focal point of a meeting between team members or between the student and facilitator. The people attending a retention meeting can devote five minutes to retention monitoring and evaluation. During this time they can reflect on these questions:

● What is going well with the retention plan?
● What is not going well with the retention plan?
● What should we do differently in order to make the retention plan effective?

These questions themselves are evaluative. They will increase the sensitivity of each team member including the student and facilitator to potential changes that need to be made in the spirit of the improvement of the student's retention plan and programme.

Sally and her facilitator make monitoring and evaluation a consistent focus of their meeting agenda. They examine the action steps each party takes to implement the retention plan, evaluate outcome and appraise the overall plan. By doing this each session, they are not taken by surprise and have built into the helping process an early-warning tracking system. The facilitator invests a considerable amount of effort in tracking Sally's progress, and in making sure that retention work is more proactive than reactive.

PRACTICE VII: CLOSURE AND LINKAGE

The achievement of the retention aim does not lead to termination of the relationship with the student. A comprehensive approach to the facilitation of retention requires sensitivity to the change process and to 'keeping the door open' if a student requires help in the future.

But once the retention aim is achieved, it is time for the student and facilitator to make a critical decision. Is it time for the student to move on in his or her academic work? It is time for the student to be more autonomous in his or her academic work? Perhaps it is not, and it is appropriate to formulate a new retention plan that allows the facilitator and student to continue their collaborative work.

However, when it is time for the student to move on in his or her academic career, facilitator and student should put closure on their work together. This closure offers them an opportunity to revisit the work they have done, what was achieved and the progress the student made, particularly in mastering the role of student in higher or post-secondary education. The closure process lends itself to this kind of summative, retrospective and concurrent review. 'Summative' means taking a look at all the work that the facilitator, student and team members undertook to promote the success of the student. By retrospective is meant looking back to see how the helping process unfolded for the student. And by concurrent is meant looking at the present, and the status of the student in relationship to his or her academic, career and personal aspirations.

Retrospective and concurrent review can be linked together for the student. The closure process can focus on students' current attitudes toward higher education, their motivation to succeed, their knowledge of institutional and non-institutional resources, and the competencies they have gained that are useful to performing effectively and successfully in the role of student. Helping students to understand the processes they undertook to achieve these outcomes can help them to gain insight into how they can master their situations in the future. In other words, the retention process serves as a personal model for how students can approach challenges in higher education as they unfold in subsequent academic experiences.

Placing closure on the retention experience raises questions about what students need or desire as they move through the next phases of their education. Certainly the retention process does not help students to resolve all the issues they face. The retention process itself may have kindled the desire for additional developmental experiences. Students may want to engage in career development counselling, or continue to augment their academic skills in areas that the retention process only helped them to master at a basic level of proficiency. The facilitator can help students to identify these needs, assess them, identify relevant opportunities and link to the appropriate resource.

It is likely that the retention helping process forges a positive bond between the facilitator and the student, and that the student will seek out the facilitator in the future for additional reassurance, support and assistance. The facilitator is prepared for this, and anticipates it as a normal part of the process of helping. The facilitator will probably set some expectations about follow-up and perhaps schedule a handful of follow-up sessions with the student over the three to six months after closure. The scheduling of these meetings suggests to students that the facilitator remains interested and available and that the student is not alone in his or her quest to master the student role. Some students will say that they do not need these follow-up meetings, but the facilitator can reframe them as opportunities to stay in touch, engage in friendly visiting or just keep up with what is happening in college. Most students, however, will concur that these meetings are useful and relevant, and will recognize them as an opportunity to stay in touch with someone who helped them to make substantial progress in their educational careers.

CONCLUSION AND GUIDELINES

The helping process is essential to any programme of retention. Its importance lies in the reality that the helping process links two or more people into a working relationship. Students are able to come into contact with a 'real person' who is devoted to their success as students in higher education. Up to the point of meeting the retention facilitator, students may have had no meaningful personal relationships with anyone in authority who could muster the resources and supports students need to address the very real issues they face. It is these issues that may disrupt their involvement in higher education.

Teaching staff may seem remote to students. Indeed, students may have no personal contact with teaching staff other than in large lectures. Teaching assistants may seem brusque, preoccupied with their own survival and their own work. Counselling staff may be interested only in the mechanics of registration and the students' choice of subject. Who is available to students to identify their issues? Who will help them to organize these issues, prioritize them and address the ones that are essential to the achievement of persistence? There is a view that responsibility lies with students themselves.

Such an attitude or belief is not conducive to keeping students in higher education. The helping process requires us to think of student retention and persistence as a collaborative process that helps the student and facilitator to form a strong relationship to achieve retention- and persistence-relevant outcomes. The helping process erects a bridge between the student and an institutional representative, someone who can get things done and who can identify and organize resources to resolve the issues the student faces. The helping process also builds a bridge between institutional expectations and student aspirations. Persistence requires students to address these expectations and meet them successfully, and not to either deny or ignore them.

Persistence also requires the institution to be responsive to its students, to take their aspirations seriously and to meet those needs or resolve those issues so students can fulfil their aspirations. An effective helping process enables students to integrate expectations and aspirations so they can achieve the outcomes they seek in their education.

Part IV
Conclusion

12

Developing the retention programme: an exemplar

MAIN POINTS OF THE CHAPTER

- This chapter introduces the First-Year Student Development Programme (FYSDP) as a composite of several different programmes that we use to illustrate the practices outlined in the book.
- The illustrative exemplar focuses on 'at-risk' students who are new to higher education. The programme defines risk using specific criteria that enables it to specify the characteristics of the students it seeks to engage.
- Criteria defining risk involve secondary school results, composition of secondary school courses, and the educational and economic status of family members and the community from which students come to university.
- The illustrative programme helps students to master the role of student within the context of a traditional university.
- The scope of the programme is quite broad, and includes student readiness and self-understanding, academic development, personal and social development, and professional and career development.
- Students receive from the programme 'enhanced' tutorials, information meetings, group support, and clarification of university expectations and requirements of students.
- Staff members prioritize relationship formation with students and they become sources of knowledge, information and practical assistance for students at the beginning of their educational careers.

- The leadership of the programme reaches out to academic administrators and teaching staff to obtain their commitment and support.
- Students have opportunities to appraise their academic needs and to obtain assistance to meet the needs they identify.
- Programme staff work with each student to help him or her develop socially and personally not only to supplement academic experience but also to identify strengths and interests that may have vocational significance to the student.
- Programme staff members also focus on vocational and career development, and they advocate for students to identify and fulfil their interests through the embellishment of their academic courses.
- The programme is physically housed in an accessible location and co-located with other student services. Flexible hours add to the accessibility of the programme.
- The programme is linked to other retention programmes, giving it a collaborative character.
- The programme has a strong image as a strengths-based and proactive resource to incoming students.
- The helping process incorporates a goal-driven and planned approach to retention that incorporates a variety of helping roles staff members use to facilitate retention.
- An outcome management approach to service provision focuses the attention of staff members, students and programme leaders on student retention and persistence outcomes.

In this chapter we highlight the various practices of a retention programme through the use of an illustrative example. The example is a composite of several different retention programmes that we have observed in the United States, including one on the campus of a four-year college the mission of which lies predominantly in undergraduate education, another at a two-year community college, and a programme that is based in a school of social work. We take the 'best practices' of each one of these and synthesize them into the illustrative example using the framework developed in the book.

This chapter introduces another colleague who is working with us in the area of retention and we incorporate into it a number of the ideas she has tried through her practice as a retention specialist. Vanessa Bard works with incoming first-year students in the setting of a four-year public university in the United States. The university considers some first-year students to be 'at risk' if they typically are the first in their families to attend higher education, they have limited financial resources and their academic preparation is weak from the standpoint of their secondary school grades and whether they completed college preparatory courses. Vanessa works with these students during their first year to promote their 'mastery of the student role' and to help them achieve the success they need to continue to the second year and stay enrolled in undergraduate education.

SELECTION OF STUDENTS AND THE SCOPE OF THE RETENTION PROGRAMME

We call our illustrative programmatic example the 'First-Year Student Development Programme'. The mission of the programme is to reach out to students who are academically at risk in their first year of undergraduate education to keep them enrolled and moving forward in their education. These students tend to be undecided about their educational purpose and direction, and ambivalent about their involvement in higher or post-secondary education although they do understand its importance to them personally from the perspective of career advancement.

As with many retention programmes its scope is quite broad, involving the four areas of student development outlined in Chapter 7. These areas are student readiness and self-understanding, academic development, personal and social development, and professional and career development. The programme seeks to organize the experiences, opportunities and supports students require to achieve success in an academic setting with which they are likely to be unfamiliar.

The programme reaches out yearly to incoming first-year students and identifies those who meet its criteria of 'at risk', which is determined through grade averages, the composition of courses the student tried and completed in secondary education, and the educational and economic status of family members, especially parents. The latter two criteria are especially important to the appropriate identification of students. These two indicators reveal the likelihood of whether students are familiar with the requirements of higher education, and whether they have available role models who can interpret the experience of higher education to them.

In addition, the economic resources of the family offer an indicator of how stressful higher education will be for students. The availability of finances will influence whether students will need to struggle to obtain financial resources, balance work and study, and extend the period of education through needing to move in and out of the workforce to earn the money they require to finance their education. Family support is another important aspect of a student's situation, so programme staff are very interested in the understanding family members have of the student's situation, the availability of family to support the student and the level of commitment the student's family has to his or her completion of higher education.

The selection of students is undertaken in a very careful and supportive manner. Programme staff do not want to label or stigmatize students. They do want to make sure that students understand the availability of the programme and the resources available to them. The orientation these students receive is especially important since they get an in-depth understanding of the four features of the programme. They get an understanding of the possibilities that higher education holds for them.

Readiness

But they should also be aware of their *readiness* to begin their careers as students. The scope of the programme incorporates a readiness dimension in which students have an opportunity to appraise their preparation (personally, socially, academically and in terms of career development) for higher education. The programme tells all its students that this self-appraisal process is neither to discourage them nor to screen them out as suitable students. Indeed, the programme tells them the opposite. The programme's message is that it is important to be aware of the student's resources and needs in terms of preparation and readiness, so as to be able to lay out a plan during the student's first term to address the needs and plan for the use of resources.

The programme arranges experiences for its students that for other students might occur informally. For example, students receive group or individual tutorials on the campus, the resources of the campus, and the university's expectations and requirements for all students. Students work individually and in groups to clarify their needs and to match these with the resources of the campus. Carefully planned social events build group cohesion and introduce group support early in the process so that students have a reference group to relate to on campus. It is important to the programme during this process of developing readiness and self-understanding that no student feels alone or experiences isolation. Students have someone to contact and form a relationship with.

Members of the programme staff emphasize the importance and practicality of readiness and self-understanding. The staff members want students to be thinking from the start of their roles as students, their understanding of their needs, and the resources available to them to meet these needs. They want students to have a support system and someone they can relate to. Staff members and students alike note that the programme is relationship-driven. Students see staff members as caring, warm and considerate, committed to student welfare and, most importantly, as sources of knowledge, information and practical assistance for students who need to resolve issues or concerns that can prevent them from realizing success if these issues or concerns go unresolved.

The 'Wednesday night dinner' is a weekly event that is well attended by students. As the students progress in the programme they begin to see themselves as members of a group devoted to the support of new students. The dinner offers an informal social setting in which students get together and share experiences. The staff members are present to discuss issues with students, and there is an information session built into the evening.

The programme devotes a considerable amount of effort to the development of student readiness since its students need this kind of support and assistance. The programme sees the first year of the student's academic experience as a 'sensitive period' during which students need socialization into the student role, require support, need information and guidance, and need opportunities to address and fulfil their concerns and issues. The programme launches its approach to helping students through relationship-based and individualized services and support.

The leadership of the programme reaches out to academic administrators and key teaching staff to secure their commitment to the readiness aspect of the programme. The programme has packaged the 'development of readiness' as a credit-bearing course so that students feel they can invest energy into strengthening their readiness for higher education. The course, 'Making higher education work for you', allows students to earn up to three academic credits in the first year. Students must complete academic assignments that help them: 1) appraise their needs as students and the resources available to them to meet these needs; 2) identify what higher education means to them; 3) obtain a basic understanding of university life; 4) analyse the role of student; and 5) examine their purpose and direction as students.

Academic development

As students participate in activities that strengthen their readiness, the programme focuses on the identification and fulfilment of their *academic development* needs. The programme takes a 'core competency' approach to ensuring that each student has basic competencies to engage in what programme staff members refer to as 'the new literacies'. These are the following five competencies:

1. Basic skills in college-level reading where academic specialists help students to assess whether they know how to read a considerable amount of material in an economical but effective manner. Students learn how to scan, search and organize reading material to get the essence of it. They learn how to appraise their assignments and then develop a reading strategy to fulfil their assignments.
2. Basic skills in the use of computer technology where academic specialists help students to become comfortable with computers, and learn the use of productivity-based software including word processing, spreadsheets and databases, and how to employ Web-based resources to access library resources and information.
3. Basic skills in numeracy where students have the opportunities to revisit, relearn or learn for the first time quantitative approaches to reasoning and problem analysis. Academic specialists help students to identify their numeracy needs in relation to core curriculum requirements and to acquire these basic skills.

4. Basic understanding of the scientific method and its use in the physical, biological and social sciences. Students receive exposure to both deductive and inductive thinking and how they can incorporate these approaches within a problem-solving framework.
5. Basic skills in presenting ideas through writing. Students have opportunities to exercise these skills through computer technology, group writing assignments, and group processing of writing.

The programme does not teach an alternative curriculum, but there are seminars, workshops and individualized learning experiences available through the programme where students can link to academic specialists, specialized academic development programmes, and tutors. The programme takes an interest in the courses its students are taking and in helping them use these courses to exercise the multiple literacies they must acquire to be successful in their roles as students.

Programme staff use the academic development area to track student performance and involvement in higher education. They emphasize the development of trust with each student and the creation of a strong relationship. The programme will ask students for permission to track their performance so that they can intervene when needed. Some students regard this tracking as intrusive. Other students regard it as something that can be tolerated if it will help them to be successful in their first year. Still other students see it as a positive feature, something that can help them stay on top of their work because they know that they may be in jeopardy of straying from their path.

The risk status of students does require oversight of their academic performance so that the programme can serve students more effectively in this area of their development. The labelling of students as 'at risk' and in need of tracking does present some ethical concerns about privacy, identification and stigmatization, autonomy and self-determination. The programme addresses these issues by working closely with an advisory council of student participants who help formulate and evaluate the tracking policy and establish procedures for its proper use. There is a consensus among programme staff that involving students in their own self-monitoring not only produces information useful to retention but also keeps students aware of their own performance.

Programme staff work closely with students to monitor and celebrate academic outcomes. The programme tracks these outcomes so that students are aware of their performance and there is considerable celebration when students complete major benchmarks of performance like examinations and course requirements. The programme's mastery approach to the student role identifies common benchmarks of performance during the course of the first year, and staff who work with students maintain a focus on these benchmarks. For example, they know just how important the first examinations are to their students' feelings of mastery, so they pay considerable attention to the preparation of their students for these examinations.

Personal and social development

The programme is very sensitive to the undergraduate years as a period where the opportunities for *personal and social development* are great. Programme staff frame these years as a period in which students who are not strong academically can still emerge as vital young adults with a clear sense of who they are and how they want to lead their lives. The programme does invest in the organization of these opportunities through social involvement, the exploration of extra-curricular activities, political involvement and the formation of personal relationships that can survive a lifetime. The areas of readiness and academic development are fused with content pertaining to personal and social development. Students have an opportunity to define themselves, to identify their needs and preferences and to discover themselves.

Students educate programme staff because members of the staff are willing to listen to their students. Some students want to complete college but do not see themselves as scholars. They want to meet people, establish relationships and participate in activities that help define themselves socially and personally.

Vocational and professional development

The personal and social objectives of students may establish a good foundation for vocation. The programme includes an area that helps students to define themselves *vocationally and professionally*. The programme is an advocate of community service education, co-operative education and vocational mentorship opportunities through which its students (as well as other students) can also earn course credits.

The programme does offer workshops on vocational interests, career paths and career development, but the 'real' vocational development opportunities have proven to be much more popular. The programme's students want opportunities to learn about the 'world of work', and some exposure to this world through career mentors from the community helps them to place the importance of their academic competencies into context. A student who wants to be a businessperson can get a quick reference point in the first year to understand the importance of writing letters, using quantitative information and even employing the scientific method. The programme helps students to create their own reference points that define the relevance of their educational experiences. Students often find this reference point in the world of work, vocation and career. The programme does not want to fall into 'vocationalism' where staff members are only preparing students for work, but they seek to link academic development to vocational development to increase the relevance of higher education to their students.

PLACEMENT AND SPONSORSHIP OF THE RETENTION PROGRAMME

The placement of the First-Year Student Development Programme (FYSDP) within the organizational structure of the college was no accident. University and programme staff gave good thought to the placement of the programme. They wanted it to be 'at street level' so that students would have ready access to the centre by walking through a welcoming entrance directly into the reception area of the programme. The physical setting of the programme is attractive and inviting to students. It is bright and well lighted. The furnishings communicate the informality of the setting, giving a homelike appearance to the programme setting.

The programme is co-located with a number of other important student services including developmental education, student associations, general student advice services, counselling and mental health services, services for students with disabilities, and student housing services. The area brings a high volume of student traffic. The array and intermingling of specialized and general student services make it difficult for most people to know that some students are coming into the complex to take advantage of a targeted and specialized retention programme. The appearance of the programme, its co-location with other student support services, and the sheer volume of activity reduce risk of the stigma that might be associated with a retention effort.

A close examination of the FYSDP reveals other important features that give the programme a collaborative sponsorship. The programme is a partnership of the college's advice and student development division, two human services agencies and several student support organizations. The advice and student development division contribute the core staffing of the programme as well as the space. The two human service agencies, a clubhouse for people in recovery from psychiatric disability and a comprehensive rehabilitation agency, each make two full-time equivalent positions available to work at the programme. These staff members, who have in-depth knowledge of local social service resources, also have skills to link students to such services. Through the outposting of these staff positions to the university the agencies facilitate access to and use of the retention programme by their own clients or members while they are also available to offer an important service to other students in the university.

Student support groups devoted to supporting women returning to work, people making the transition from state benefits to education and students with disabilities contribute to the staffing complement of the programme. Members of these student groups offer important social support, social involvement and educational opportunities to students in the FYSDP. The activities of student development staff, students involved in self-help and mutual support, and providers of human services are different, and each group contributes something different to the success of the FYSDP. By virtue of combining these different entities and their unique student support activities, the FYSDP is more than the sum of its parts. The collaborative sponsorship gives it a unique and creative flavour, and offers hope to students who may feel overwhelmed by their initial academic experience in higher education.

REACHING OUT TO STUDENTS, TEACHING STAFF AND ACADEMIC ADMINISTRATORS

The ability to reach out to university stakeholders who are critical to the success of the FYSDP is an important competence of the programme. Programme staff consider 'reaching out' as a principal responsibility that ensures not only the viability of the FYSDP but also its relevance to a diverse customer base. The broad scope of the programme ensures that students will find something of value they can relate to and put to immediate use in their academic careers. The staff members of the FYSDP are quick to identify students and to form relationships with them based on warmth, caring and commitment to their success.

The collaborative sponsorship of the programme, combined with its co-location within a matrix of student support services and its warm and informal appearance, reduces student anxiety about coming into the programme and making use of it, and reduces the stigma students may feel. These features combine to make the FYSDP highly accessible and to ensure that it serves as a practical resource to students that can produce for them immediate benefits with very little social cost.

The outreach function of the FYSDP is composed of four basic aims:

- getting the word out among students that the programme is available to incoming first-year students;
- helping teaching staff and academic administrators understand the programme and how to link students to it;
- linking to specific students who fit the FYSDP retention profile;
- engaging students and helping them identify their own way of making use of the FYSDP.

The staff and student members of the programme have formulated a strong sense of image they want to communicate to the larger university community. They fully understand the reality that the students the programme seeks to serve possess serious academic needs that may also coincide with concerns relating to economic status, absence of family support and the absence of a clear sense of what they seek to accomplish in higher education. Yet FYSDP students possess many strengths and assets that can facilitate their success in higher education.

Programme staff and student members communicate a strengths perspective focusing on helping students to learn about the student role and how to master it.

They convey information about the programme through flyers, electronic advertising, bulletin board announcements and class announcements directly to students. The programme has a marketing group composed of student members and programme staff that is responsible for communicating the programme's message. The group manages a speakers' bureau, and sends students and programme staff as small teams to teaching staff and departmental meetings to get the message to key staff members, particularly those who teach the main first-year subjects. Members of the speakers' bureau are regular contributors to the university's orientation course for new teaching staff and academic administrators. The aim of the programme is to get its message out proactively and to communicate a hopeful and positive message about how students can succeed in using their strengths, addressing their needs and managing their educational careers.

The FYSDP has built a strong connection to the admissions unit of the college. The programme has developed and maintains a student contact list of all students who meet the criteria of the FYSDP. Programme staff use these databases to contact students with their positive message. Students are invited to attend a dinner where they can obtain further information about the FYSDP, which offers an opportunity to ask questions about what the programme can offer them. The programme tries to link to students coming from many different educational backgrounds. A challenge for the programme is not to over-market its services by reaching out to too many students. Programme staff are always trying to balance their capacity to serve students with the number that need the FYSDP services and supports.

The most powerful outreach approach comes in the form of one-to-one marketing where the FYSDP representative meets a small group of students or one student at a time. The representative tailors an invitation to the student that is in the context of the student's own experience in education. The representative relates stories about how other students made use of the FYSDP and with their own strengths and assets combined with those of the programme overcame obstacles to achieve success in higher education. A key programme practice is to begin relationship formation with students at the point of outreach.

The programme follows up referrals by teaching staff and inquiries by students. FYSDP staff members assume that once students hear about the programme they will begin to contemplate their use of it. Some students will act quickly to link to the programme while others will take their time. Programme staff work with students of differing motivations and in differing emotional states. Those who link early will probably experience a decrease in their anxiety levels while those who wait may come to the programme feeling considerable stress about their current academic situations. Many students postpone contacting the FYSDP until they face an academic crisis, and so the programme has improved its capacity to track students and reach out to them, for example by inexpensive methods like e-mail or greetings cards.

Good outreach can create awareness but students will make use of their awareness in different ways and at different times. Thus, the FYSDP is prepared to work with students in whatever state they present themselves. This flexible attitude on the part of the programme is a product of their commitment to the programme's mission. They want to help students to achieve success in the first year and are willing to engage a student when he or she seeks help.

FYSDP HELPING PROCESS AND RETENTION ROLES

The FYSDP prides itself in the ability of its staff members to form strong and enduring relationships with the first-year students it seeks to retain. All services are driven by this strong orientation to relationship building that pervades the programme and all its services. Initial contacts with students focus on relationship development that dovetails into a focus on the development of student readiness and self-understanding. For example, an FYSDP staff member working with an individual student or small group of students gets to know the students as people. The staff member invests time to identify their aspirations from a personal and career perspective, and to obtain an understanding of their families and the expectations their families have about their involvement in post-secondary or higher education.

The development of the relationship is time well invested. The understanding the FYSDP staff member forms of each student helps the staff member and student to collaborate on the formation of a retention aim or goal. The FYSDP understands the importance of getting this in place, helping the student to frame it and getting each student to understand the importance of persistence and retention. With the goal in place, the FYSDP helps students to assess their readiness for post-secondary or higher education, the supports they require and the barriers they must overcome or remove. FYSDP retention plans are a synthesis of the retention goal, the assessment, and the actions the students and staff members must undertake to foster readiness, increase supports and remove barriers.

With the plans in place, FYSDP students and staff members work on implementation of the action steps. The implementation is monitored, and the actions of staff members and students are tracked. The plans are not rigid. Students and staff members can recommend changes or modifications based on their experience of the implementation of the plan. The FYSDP programme values relevance of the plan over its formalism.

The plan offers an opportunity for staff members to engage students in a process of evaluation. Staff members work with students to judge the effectiveness of the plan in relation to the development of student readiness, supports and the reduction of barriers. In addition, staff members help students to understand the effects of their plans on their persistence, success and retention.

The staff members of the FYSDP understand that students change quickly during the process of post-secondary and higher education. Students change in terms of knowledge, skills, behaviours and attitudes, and many students become more mature adults as this helping process unfolds. Staff members frequently scrutinize their work with students using these indicators of maturation and they ensure that the plans will change as students change in maturity and in aspirations.

But the real drama of the FYSDP helping process unfolds as staff members use various helping roles. The FYSDP invests considerable resources in the development of student readiness, and much of this work is undertaken by staff members who serve as counsellors, interpreters, and guides for groups. The programme offers a highly structured but informal curriculum that helps students to learn about the resources of the university. Staff members guide students through structured exercises that help them to work with one another in learning about the university and the student role.

FYSDP staff members spend a considerable amount of time as resource developers. The programme prides itself in being able to fashion resources for each student. For example, a student who was at risk of losing her student housing place because of drug use was able to enter a university treatment programme. The FYSDP staff member developed this opportunity and as a troubleshooter mediated between the director of residential services and the student to ensure that both parties could negotiate a solution to what emerged as a conflict-laden impasse. FYSDP staff members often find that resource development and troubleshooting go hand in hand. This is not surprising. Defeating a barrier (eg losing a student housing place) and creating a resource (eg entry into a chemical dependency treatment programme) characterize a lot of the retention work of the FYSDP.

OUTCOME MANAGEMENT

All of the work of the FYSDP comes together around the idea of outcome management. The staff members of the programme do not want to hold on to a student too long. Nor do they wish to be too intrusive into the lives of students. However, their accountability lies in offering the right amount of service and support to help students to move forward in their careers in post-secondary and higher education.

Thus, the programme incorporates a template of outcomes that help staff members to monitor their overall delivery of retention services. There are 10 principal performance outcomes and the staff members of the programme manage these outcomes purposively and monitor them as a team in a tenacious manner. These outcomes are:

1. students' knowledge of their roles and responsibilities in higher education;
2. students' attendance patterns throughout the first year;

3. teaching staff ratings of the students' work in each course;
4. students' interim grades in the first year;
5. students' final grades for each course and the completion of each course;
6. students' timely start to each term of the first year;
7. students' registration for the second year;
8. acceptable overall average grades in the first year;
9. students' satisfaction with their educational course;
10. resolution of all crises or issues that can disrupt persistence.

The utilization review committee of the programme oversees key performance outcomes and demands evidence in each situation about how the student is progressing in relationship to these performance outcomes. The effectiveness of utilization review is a direct outcome of the information management system that is one of the FYSDP's greatest assets.

The quality management committee of the programme oversees the formulation, use and evaluation of best practice standards, and conducts regular audits of student cases to ensure that staff members incorporate these practices in relationship to programme outcomes. Thus the programme seeks to bring together outcome management, utilization review, quality management and information into a system that facilitates the individual and administrative monitoring of its work.

CONCLUSION AND GUIDELINES

This chapter brings into relief the operation of an illustrative programme that incorporates the various dimensions that we outlined in previous chapters. The programme has its own purpose, character and style, and incorporates best practices in its own way rather than following these in a rigid manner. Best practices serve as a framework within which a retention programme can exercise a great deal of creativity and innovation. In other words, it is up to the members of the retention programme, whether staff, students, administrators or supporters, to decide about the relative mix and emphasis of various practices.

A retention programme has its own conception, purpose and aims that build on the institutional mission of retention and make use of the infrastructure of retention the institution offers its students and staff. The design of the retention programme is purposeful, and designers articulate its major features according to their theory of retention.

The FYSDP, for example, is developmental in its orientation. Designers understand that the previous experiences of some students create a need for enhanced persistence and retention services for these students. The designers do not want to meet this need in a manner that sets the students apart from the general student body. Nor do they want to create stigma. They want to nest the retention programme into the range of services the university offers to all its students and, therefore, they make purposeful decisions about the location, appearance, accessibility and availability of the programme. The designers do not want students to feel isolated, so they emphasize the building of a community in which student development is the focus of the work of the community membership that encompasses students, teaching staff, programme staff members and administrators. The FYSDP, as a consequence, invests greatly in communal events like the weekly dinner, group meetings and group activities.

The illustrative example communicates the intentions of the designers. They seek to develop their students and do so in a collaborative and meaningful way. Retention is not merely 'keeping students in higher education'. It is also about helping each student develop as a successful student who is navigating (perhaps with some bumps) some of the most important years of adult life.

Index

academic curricula   72
academic development
   and readiness of students   183–84
   infrastructure of 119–20
   programmatic characteristics in
      retention   120
academic maturity   93–94
academic options
   decisions about   23
   student awareness of   108
academic skills
   assessment of   151
   importance of   5
access of students to retention services
   80–82, 143–45
adult education   37–39
advocacy   155–56
aspirations of students   163–64
assessor role in retention service
   151
at-risk criteria   181–82
awareness of retention need   77–80

career
   development   37
   educational careers   36–37
   exploration   87
   mobility and change   37
   transition   38

closure of retention helping process
   173–75
collaborative sponsorship of retention
   features of successful collaboration
      131–32, 187
   overview   129–31
co-location of retention programme
   173–75
communities and retention   59
community service education   72
connecting to students   141–43
continuing professional development
   37–39
counsellor role in retention   149–50
crisis intervenor role in retention
   154–55

diversity
   importance to retention   59
   of educational careers   36–37
   of educational opportunities
      33–34
   of higher education   4, 37
   of retention assets   59
   of student demographics   34–36
   of student government   64–70
   of students   4–5

emotional support of students   28, 99